PROCLAIMING
CHRIST
TODAY

PROCLAIMING CHRIST TODAY

W. Norman Pittenger

THE
Seabury Press

GREENWICH · CONNECTICUT · 1962

© 1962 by The Seabury Press, Incorporated
Library of Congress Catalog Card Number: 62-9616
375-1261-C-3.5
Printed in the United States of America

PREFACE

For one whose whole ministry has been spent in theological teaching it may seem presumptuous to speak on the subject of preaching. Those who minister regularly in the Church's congregations have a much more immediate experience of what it means to be a preacher than do those of us who are engaged in academic work. Yet it may be that, entirely apart from the preaching of the gospel in which any theological teacher does in fact from time to time engage outside the walls of his school, his experience in teaching those who are to be clergy of the Church, and in my case a special concern for the "apologetic" of "gospelling," can be of use to those who are in the parish ministry or are soon to enter it, and who are now or soon will be forced to consider with utmost seriousness the obligation in this matter of preaching the gospel which their ordination lays upon them.

The chapters of this book are in substance the lectures delivered in Australia, during my visit to that country in the autumn of 1959. Either in full or in part, they were delivered at St John's College, Morpeth, New South Wales; St Mark's Collegiate Library, Canberra, A.C.T.; the University of Queensland, Brisbane, Queensland; and before meetings, sponsored by the Australian Council for the World Council of Churches, held in Brisbane, Melbourne, and Sydney.

They have also served as the basis for a series of lectures which I have delivered during the past several years in the United States and in Canada—in Maryland, Delaware, North Dakota, California, Oregon, Hawaii, Washington, D.C., and at Huron College in London, Ontario. Chapter V is based on a lecture which was given at Yale Divinity School several years ago, in connection with a symposium on Christian Worship.

To the many clergymen who attended the conferences in the United States and Canada, at which I delivered the lectures; to those who so patiently listened to them in Australia; and to the friends who made the arrangements for these several occasions, I am deeply grateful. I should like especially to thank the trio of former students of mine from Australia who so kindly welcomed me, entertained me, and worked out the program of my travels 'down under': the Right Reverend John C. Vockler, Bishop of Mount Gambier; the Reverend Gordon D. Griffith, Vice-Principal of St John's College, Morpeth; and the Reverend David M. Taylor, Secretary of the Australian Council for the World Council of Churches. It is impossible to list separately the many leaders in the Christian Church in Australia, of all denominations, who were so generous to me during my stay in their country; but I thank them with all my heart for all that they did to make my visit memorable and pleasant. I must also make special mention of Dr. and Mrs. Clarence I. Benson of Port Deposit, Maryland, for their kindnesses when I gave these lectures in the Episcopal diocese of Easton.

W. NORMAN PITTENGER

The General Theological Seminary,
New York City

CONTENTS

[handwritten annotations: "Jesus", "The Church", "Sinners", "Eucharist"]

1.
THE
GOSPEL
WE
PROCLAIM

Why is it that so much preaching today is without power? The answer to this question cannot be found, as is so often claimed, in the inadequacies of the preacher so far as his rhetorical skill, his use of apt illustrations, his logical development of theme, and so forth are in view. These are important matters, of course; and no minister should venture into the pulpit without adequate preparation for his task, the use of whatever elocutionary techniques he can learn, and the employment of the pointed illustration which will bring his sermon to life for his hearers. But the real explanation of our ineffectual preaching lies much deeper: far too many of us, far too much of the time, do not recognize the terrible truth that as preachers we are engaged in nothing other than the task of confronting our listeners with the very Word of God. We do not recognize sufficiently clearly that in the human words which we use our listeners are to hear not so much what *we* say, as what *God* says to them through us. We do not see with sufficient clarity that, as those who have been set apart by Christ in his Church for the work of the ministry, we are "stewards of the mysteries of God," who are commissioned to bring his Word or revelation to his people and in his name to pronounce the message of salvation.

All too much of the time we consider our preaching to be an exercise in theological teaching, in moral exhortation, or in pious meditation. There is room for each of these in our ministry, but none of these things is what is meant by *preaching the gospel*. It matters not whether we be conservative or liberal, traditionalist or modernist; in whatever category we may be placed, or place ourselves, the fact remains that insofar as we are Christian ministers, ordained by Christ in his Church to be his ministering agents, our *preaching* can be nothing other than the proclamation of God's Word for the wholeness of men. And once this recognition is at the heart of our ministry, our preaching will become effectual—not that we are ever more than unworthy and "unprofitable" servants, but that God in Christ can and does use our unworthiness for his own great ends and makes even our imperfections to serve him.

Confusion of the preaching office of the ministry with the work of the pastor as teacher has been a bad thing and has produced bad results; for no sermon is long enough to be, nor is its purpose properly envisaged as, an exercise in teaching. On the other hand, the confusion of the two tasks has often meant that the significance of the proclamation of the "Word of God" has been lost sight of in the valid concern for the ministry of teaching.

When a man is ordained to the sacred ministry in any of the Reformed churches—and this includes the Anglican Communion, which even the staunchest defenders of its "catholicity" must acknowledge is a "reformed" catholic communion—a form of words is used in which the centrality of the preaching office in that ministry is affirmed. It was customary among the Reformers themselves to speak of a "valid" ministry as one in which "the pure Word of God is preached and the sacraments be duly administered according to Christ's ordinance" (to quote the Anglican Thirty-nine Articles, which are parelleled in other and similar "confessions"); and the history of the ministry in the Christian Church as a whole makes it abundantly clear that "authority to preach the Word of God," or the right to "dispense the Word of God," or the giving to the candidate of the Church's recognition and authority to be "preacher of the Gospel" —all these are more or less synonymous phrases—has been an integral part of ordination.

There are many differences between the various Christian bodies which emerged from the Reformation in the sixteenth century—differences in theology and differences in order —but the importance of the preaching office is one point in which they agree. All of them insist that among the functions of an ordained man, one of the most important roles, although not the only important one, is that he is to preach the "Word of God" which is the gospel of our Lord Jesus Christ.

The minister certainly is not *only* a preacher; and we may regret that many who ought to know better have been content to use that one word to describe his work. The administration of the Church's sacraments is equally important, of course, and this is especially true for us if we accept the position of the sixteenth-century Reformers that in the celebration of the sacraments of Baptism and Holy Communion, as well as in the pulpit, the gospel is proclaimed and expressed. In fact, we may rightly claim that the preaching of the gospel and the administration of the sacraments must necessarily go together; to put it in language used by Professor Whitehead in *Religion in the Making*, the "cult" (by which Whitehead meant the social action of worship) and the "myth" (by which he meant the story which explains a society's worship) can never be separated. It is the intimate and indissoluble union of the two which prevents preaching from becoming merely a hortatory exercise or a public address, and which prevents the sacrament from becoming merely routine with suggestions which might seem to border on "magic."

The pulpit is the place for the declaration of the Word of God and not the place for teaching Christian theology or the principles of Christian morality, although it is obvious that the gospel of Christ has theological implications and involves moral consequences. One of the failures of the ministry today is a tendency to forget that the minister as preacher is *primarily* and *essentially* concerned with this task, however much other matters may engage his interest on other occasions and in other aspects of his work. A clergyman functions as a preacher when he proclaims Christ, the significance of Christ for men, and the need for acceptance of Christ as bringing wholeness of life; he is to preach for repentance and for participation in the Church which is the setting for the gospel. Of course he will do all this in many different ways. My point is that he is not to look upon himself, *in his function as preacher*, as a teacher or as a director of souls or as a theological lecturer. It is a mistake to use the *pulpit* for what we might describe as didactic purposes, however important and necessary the task of teaching may be in other connections.

We have been speaking of "the gospel." What *is* this gospel which we are to preach? Before attempting to answer this question, I should like to make some highly important preliminary distinctions, by saying what the gospel is *not*. Often we can come to the positive truth by considering and rejecting inadequate or false ideas, and perhaps nowhere is this so useful as in the subject we have under consideration.

First of all, the gospel is *not* simply the teaching of Jesus, particularly when this is understood as denoting his religious and moral admonitions and exhortations. There can be no doubt, of course, that the teaching of our Lord is of enormous significance, not only for its own intrinsic value but also because it enables us to understand the kind of person that Jesus himself was, humanly speaking. Many years ago, Dr. Frank Russell Barry, the present Bishop of Southwell, wrote a book entitled *The Relevance of Christianity*. In that book he made the point that the teaching of Jesus— his words as reported to us in the New Testament—has its peculiar importance for us in that it shows "who Jesus was" in terms of "what Jesus said." As we all know, it is frequently possible for us to determine a man's character, his quality of life, his way of being a man, by listening to what he has to say. We comment about him that he is the *sort of man* who says things like that. In the case of Abraham Lincoln, for example, it was not only the things that Lincoln did, but it was also the things that he said and (in this modern instance) the things that he wrote in letters and state papers, which make it possible for us to know the kind of man that he really was. And when the words that a man says are confirmed by the testimony of a life in agreement with them, we may well come to know that man and his personal quality in a very deep and real way. So it is with Jesus.

Yet it remains true that the gospel, the good news which the Church proclaims, is not in itself simply what Jesus said. What he said may be paralleled very largely in the teaching of the rabbis of his time and later. As Wellhausen once remarked, everything that Jesus said (save, I think, his teaching about God's "seeking the lost") can be found in the highest and best Jewish teaching; although Wellhausen had to add that much more may be found in this teaching which Jesus eliminated or rejected—our Lord's human genius here, if the word may be used, was in his selectivity. But it is still the fact that the early Church did not go out into the world proclaiming the teaching of a great Jewish rabbi. It remembered and taught what Jesus had said about God and man, about the kingdom of God, about human moral responsibility, and the like, because it was *primarily* concerned with something else. That something else gave the teaching its importance; it was not the other way round.

Again, the gospel is not a statement of theological propositions. It is indeed inevitable that the Church should develop a theology, a structure of beliefs which are drawn from, and seek to state in as precise language as possible, the gospel and its significance for men. Those who loudly proclaim that they have no theology and that they desire none are all the more likely to have an *implicit* theology—and doubtless it will be a bad one, since it is not consciously held and therefore is not open to continued critical examination. But no

eology, whether that of a Barth or of a Brunner, even that
f an Augustine or an Aquinas, a Luther or a Calvin, or even
at of a Paul, if he can be said to have had *a* theology, can
ke the place of the gospel itself. The gospel comes before
l these theologies and is the basis for their determination
s well as the criterion of their validity. This is why there is
danger in what is often described as "doctrinal preaching."
ll too frequently this turns out to be a substitution for the
spel; it consists of some set of propositions, however tra-
tional and however true they may be, which can in fact ob-
ure the basic affirmations of Christian faith and make the
spel itself of none effect for those who hear. A theology
e must have, and it should be the best theology that is
vailable for us, carefully constructed and critically under-
ood; but we must not make the mistake of thinking that
hen we have enunciated and then expounded some theo-
gical proposition, be it from the golden middle ages or
om Karl Barth, we have thereby communicated the gospel
 the living God.

Finally, the gospel is not to be confused with creedal and
nfessional formulations. It was right that the Church
ould have come to state its basic faith in such terms as we
d in the historical creeds; but the faith which the gospel
okes, and the gospel which evokes that faith, cannot be
ntained in the historical formulations, even though it is
ated in them. Here it is necessary, of course, to make a
stinction between the later developed creeds—and above
l, the various "confessions of faith" of the Reformation
riod—and the Apostles' Creed. The latter admittedly
mes much closer to being a "gospel statement." And be-
nd that creed, we can see that the *primitive* "confessions of

faith," to which Professor Cullman has lately drawn our a
tention, are the almost immediate result of the proclaimin
of the gospel itself. "Jesus is the Lord," "Jesus is the Me.
siah," "Jesus the Messiah is the Son of God": here we con
very close to the gospel, or we already have it stated for u
We can see how the Apostles' Creed is an extension or e:
pansion of such "confessions," made necessary because (
movements of thought or opinion which were beginning 1
invade the Christian community and to threaten the inte,
rity of the gospel the Church preached. We can see, to(
how the Nicene Creed, although more theological in n:
ture, is a further amplification to meet further dangers. B
even so it remains true that what we might style "creed
preaching" is not the same thing as preaching the gospel i
self.

If, then, the gospel is not the moral and religious teachin
of Jesus, not a theological system, and not the creeds ar
confessions of the Church, what is it? The answer is real
very simple and yet very profound. The gospel is nothin
other than the proclamation of Jesus Christ himself, in tl
fullness of his historic human life among us, apprehende
and declared as the definitive and focal operation of God
the affairs of men. The gospel is nothing other than Jes
Christ our Lord, proclaimed to be the "way, the truth, ar
the life." It is the announcement that in him very God
manifest in very man, for us men and for our wholeness.
is the declaration that in him God "has visited and redeem
his people." Nothing other than this, nothing less than th
can claim to be the gospel which makes men wise unto s:
vation.

In our day we have been much enlightened concerni

the primitive forms in which this gospel, "the Word of God," was proclaimed. Thanks especially to the critical study of Dr. C. Harold Dodd, as summed up in his notable little book *The Apostolic Preaching,* we have become familiar with the word *kerygma,* Greek for "the proclamation"; and taught by Dr. Dodd and those who have followed the line of en- quiry which he laid down, we have come to see that this *kerygma* was the very heart of the earliest Christianity. This is New Testament Christianity. We have the written "gos- pels," or accounts of Jesus' sayings and actions, because it was increasingly felt necessary to give a setting for the proc- lamation. They contain recollections, in faith, of the life of him about whom the proclamation is made; for men remem- bered what Jesus had said and what he had done because he was the subject of their proclamation. It was the proclama- tion of him as "Lord and Christ" which gave to the primitive Christian community its uniqueness and its special quality. All this is, or ought to be, common knowledge for the clergy; and increasingly it will be common knowledge for the in- structed laity too.

Not quite so frequently do we recognize the variety of ways in which this primitive Christian *kerygma* was ex- pressed by the early Christian preachers. Dr. Dodd has given us a brief summary which is very useful in stating the essential elements in that declaration: how that the God of Israel, who had spoken by the prophets, had acted decisively in Christ, pouring out the gift of the Spirit, and how that this Christ, now exalted, would return in glory for the establish- ment of God's kingdom. But there are many different ways in which this main declaration found expression, and we have many of these statements of the basic *kerygma* in the

New Testament. Sometimes they are very short indeed: "God was in Christ reconciling the world unto himself"; "while we were yet sinners, Christ died for us"; "God set forth his Son to be the propitiation for our sins"; "God so loved the world that he gave his only-begotten Son"; "the Word was made flesh and dwelt among us." Sometimes, as in many of St. Paul's epistles, they are more fully stated. But in most various phrasing and with very differing emphasis, in the light of one pattern of thought or another, the same proclamation is being made; and always it comes down to this: that in the Man Jesus, in the totality of his life and action, God has been active, God has been present, in a definitive fashion, to the end that man may have life in him. Each of the various ways of statement is by its very nature a way of apprehending this gospel and then of proclaiming it.

Now it was natural that the first Christian evangelists should proclaim Jesus against the background of Jewish thought and in the context of what they conceived to be God's historical manner of dealing with his people Israel. They knew of this dealing through what we call the Old Testament scriptures and through the continuing Jewish traditions of their time. Hence they used this material in their proclamation. This was inevitable. For our Lord did not come into the world as a kind of *deus ex machina*; "he came unto his own." He appeared as a Jew among Jews; and the Fourth Gospel rightly asserts, "salvation is of the Jews" in the sense that it is only against that background and in that context that the gospel of Christ can be known and understood. In that sense, too, Pope Pius XI was entirely right when he said that "spiritually all Christians are Semites." This is why the earliest preaching was by way of saying that in Jesus all of God's promises made to Israel were fulfilled: he is the "Yea" and the "Amen." This is why they "searched the Scriptures"—the Jewish sacred writings—to find the material which they could use as testifying and witnessing to their Lord and Master. Marcion, with his attempt to de-judaize Jesus, succeeded only in "de-historicizing" him and thereby making him of no real significance; and Tertullian, the great Christian apologist against Marcion, saw this to be the case and stated it clearly and convincingly. You cannot deracinate Jesus, removing him from his given setting in history and among his own people "after the flesh," without at the same time making him a meaningless monstrosity.

And yet, while all this is true and must be emphasized unfailingly in the Church, we cannot, on the other hand, make Jesus simply a figure with Jewish significance and interpret him only in terms of biblical patterns of thought. For when we do this we are equally in danger of reducing his place in the world. In my judgment this is the error of a great many of the exponents of what is nowadays known as "biblical theology." With all their laudable effort to understand the integrity of the Scriptures, both Old and New, and to insist on the basic unity of the Bible; with all their recognition of the place of Jesus within the setting of Jewish piety and religious thought, these scholars sometimes fail to see that the very truth about God which the Bible as a whole affirms, and above all that which the New Testament says about Jesus himself, can be smothered by sheer biblicism and thereby made meaningless for those to whom the gospel should be a living, vitalizing, and contemporary message.

In his valuable commentary *The First Epistle of St. Peter*, Professor F. W. Beare writes:

If the gospel is to win the hearts of man in any age, it must clothe itself in contemporary forms and bring into its service every thought, imagination, and aspiration of man, that is congenial to its own inner spirit. The glory of Christianity, indeed, lies in this very power to draw enrichment from every source, and to 'become all things to all men.'

That is to say, the Christian gospel, the *kerygma* or proclamation, indeed remains and must remain fixed as the message of the Church, the heart of its life and the meaning of its existence; but at the same time we must find ways in which we can both understand and declare that *kerygma* which will not smother it in an unimaginative biblicism, but which will be appropriate for our own day. We must use all our ingenuity and all our wisdom, all our sympathy and all our wit, to communicate to men and women in our time the central and basic biblical affirmation, without which there would be no Christianity at all and which we believe to be the very Word of God for the men and women of our age as of every age. We shall return to the theme at a later point.

One of the first steps towards an undertaking of the meaning of the gospel is the recognition that the language in which the *kerygma* was initially stated is metaphorical language. I do not mean by this that the gospel is merely a "fairy-tale," although it is, of course, true that such tales are often told in *language* of that kind. What I mean is that the words used *in* the telling, the story itself as told, the ideas that are being conveyed, as well as the setting in which the *kerygma* is to be seen, are not "prose" but are of the nature of poetry and symbol. Here we have imaginative language, evocative in character, not the "literal" language of the chronicle. The gospel which we proclaim is not phrased in the idiom of scientific statement, nor is it told in terms of a philosophical syllogism. It is in fact a *story* and it can be spoken about, and heard, only when this is recognized. Canon T. O. Wedel has said much the same thing in his description of the gospel as a "drama." But this does not imply and must not suggest that the gospel is not grounded in history and established upon events which actually occurred in the world of human experience.

There is an unfortunate impression, found as well among the clergy as among the laity, that to describe the gospel in such metaphorical terms is equivalent to saying that it is not true. One can only remark that it would be a good thing if such persons read a little poetry now and then. Evidently they suffer from the delusion that whatever is not put in prose must necessarily be a lie. But the truth is that in the great matters of life, we men have no choice: we *must* speak as poets. M. Jourdain was wrong; he had not been speaking "prose," but *poetry,* all his life. The heart always speaks imaginatively, poetically; and truth that is to go to the heart must be phrased in this mode. Furthermore, precisely because the gospel has to do with historical event, and because it understands that event in the light of faith in the unseen divine reality whom we call God, there is no other language available for us. To talk of history is to talk imaginatively; otherwise we are not talking about history at all, but about "chronicle" or "annal," which is a very different thing. In Germany they can distinguish between *historie,* or sheer chronicling, and *geschichte,* or event apprehended in its deep significance; in English, alas, this verbal distinction cannot be made. But the fact remains a fact, nonetheless. Significant history is always told in the imaginative idiom of poetry. And when to that plain fact we add the specifically Christian interpretation of our Lord's life, death, and rising-again, in which God is seen as involved in a supreme manner in occurrences in the public domain of history, it is all the more necessary to use imaginative language, metaphor, poetry, symbol. For we *cannot* speak literally about God and his ways, as if we had a precise chart for the purpose of mapping the divine activity. There is always likeness in difference. When St. Thomas Aquinas says, in the *Summa Theologica* (Bk. III, Qu. 8, Art. 1), that the phrase "Christ is the Head of the Church" is metaphorical, he goes on to make this important point, "In metaphorical speech we must not expect a likeness in all respects; for thus there would be not likeness but identity." In that statement he gives us a clue to the nature of theological language, and *a fortiori* to the language appropriate to the gospel: it is not precise *identity,* but *likeness,* that is in view; and this, as he notes, means that we speak, and can only speak, in metaphor. Religious language is poetical. But the fact that the language is metaphorical, or if you will poetical, does not mean that it is untrue. It does not imply that the events of which the gospel speaks did not happen.

It was of course the historicity of Jesus Christ which provided a major reason for the victory of Christian faith in the Graeco-Roman world. But we must now go on to notice that such historicity need not mean that we have a complete and carefully detailed record of our Lord's days in Palestine. We do not possess any such record. What we do have is a series of reminiscences, collected and handed on "from faith to faith." We have impressions of the impact of Jesus on those who knew him best. Our "early traditions about Jesus" (to

se the title of a little book by the late Professor Bethune-
Baker) are not interested so much in what has been called
he "biographical Jesus" as they are concerned with what
esus did and said as he was remembered by those who be-
eved him to be their Lord, the Risen Messiah, and who
vere therefore anxious to hand on to others what was re-
nembered about him.

Some scholars indeed have thought that because this is the
ase, we can have no genuine knowledge of the Jesus of his-
ory. Such scholars may be on the extreme radical wing or
ney may be extreme conservatives. The former would
nd to minimize the centrality of the historical Jesus in the
eligion named after him and would turn Christianity into
mere symbol. The latter would stress the Christ of faith
-perhaps the Christ of the Church's faith—and would feel
nat the historical life matters little in comparison to the sal-
ation wrought out in the believer's faith. But we maintain,
n the contrary, that we know the Jesus of history very well,
en if we do not have a precise and photographic account
his day-by-day activities; and the unique claim of Chris-
anity is that in and by those events in the actual realm
historical happenedness, God is revealed—revealed, of
urse, in and under the conditions of history and human life,
t revealed nonetheless. There is no Christ of faith who is
t continuous with the Jesus who walked this earth in the
st century of our era. *Jesus* is seen by faith to be the
rist; but the *Christ* is one and the same person as the Jesus
history.

Having said this, however, we must also notice what ought
any event to have been obvious: that the several gospels
collections of brief tales, remembered incidents, bits of

sayings, and the like, all gathered together in the interest
giving what St. Mark's opening words so well describe: "t
beginning of the gospel of Jesus Christ the Son of God"-
the account of the historical happenings, as the Christi
community remembered them, which gave rise to the fai
that Jesus is the promised Messiah and the divine Lord. Th
"account of the historical happenings" is not like a new
paper reporter's story of some public meeting or some inc
dent that he has been sent to "cover." The account is inev
tably "conditioned" by faith; it is seen in faith; it is commun
cated along with faith. It has its setting in what the Germa
form-critics have called the *sitz-im-leben,* the "life-situation
of the primitive Christian Church. But it has its setting als
as Professor Paul Minear has lately insisted, in the "fait
situation" and in the "worship-situation" of the Christi
community, if these barbarous terms may be allowed. N
only did the exigencies of the life of the first Christians, wi
the problems they had to face, occasion the handing on of t
tales and the teaching, and to a large degree determine ho
the tales and the teaching were to be communicated. Th
demands of faith in Jesus, which as it developed came to pen
trate ever more deeply into the meaning of his person an
work, and the requirements of the worship of God known i
faith as working in Jesus the Lord, a worship which likewis
was developing in those early days, had their part both i
the telling of the stories and in the way the stories were tol

But what importance has all this for the preaching of th
gospel? I should answer that such an understanding of th
way in which the compilation of the gospel narratives too
place, and also of the nature of the material which they con
tain, delivers us in our preaching of the *kerygma* from muc

that was troublesome and confusing to an earlier generation. Our recognition of the metaphorical language in which the gospel is couched, as well as our knowledge of how the setting of that message in the life of Christ took shape, does not in any way reduce its historicity. What is does do is help us to have a better appreciation of the material which gives us the gospel, and thus it assists us towards an approach to the preaching of the gospel which is of extraordinary value in our own day, as we shall attempt to show in a succeeding chapter.

We have been speaking of the need for finding a way of stating the *kerygma* which will be relevant to our own time, while it will also be true to the abiding affirmation of faith which gives the Church its essential being. This leads on to an emphasis on the necessity for translation. In our preaching of the gospel we must get at it, present its "offense," in such a fashion that it is a challenge to decision for men and women who live in the middle half of the twentieth century. But the idiom of the Bible, in which the gospel is phrased for us, seems unintelligible to many such persons. It is not merely that they cannot understand what we say, it is that they cannot understand what we are talking about. Hence we *must* translate; we must be ready to say, "in other words. . . ."

Now some seem to think that all translation is traduction; they would appear to assume that to translate is inevitably to betray the original. Of course, this may be so. If we are not sufficiently instructed in the original, if we do not have an ear open to nuances, if we are literal-minded and prosaic, we shall doubtless be guilty of traduction. But on the other hand, the refusal to translate at all is likely to make us sound like parrots repeating a merely verbal form to those who somehow or other can be brought to listen to such boring stuff. Of course, the fact is that translation need not necessarily be betrayal at all; it can be faithful translation. Translation, if it is to be good, involves two factors: first, that we shall know the language *from* which we translate; and second, that we shall know the language *into* which we translate. In the period now so often dismissed as "the age of liberalism," it was doubtless true that some who engaged in translation did not know, deeply and thoroughly, the language *from* which they were to translate; hence they sometimes preached a gospel which was another gospel from that which "makes" the Church. But in the present time, altogether too many of us may know or think we know the original quite well, but yet do not know the language *into* which we are to translate; hence the gospel as preached is preached to ears that do not and cannot hear, because they are ears that are attuned to a quite different set of conditions, patterns of thought, and ways of conceiving the universe.

This business of translation is unqestionably an exacting task. Probably one reason for the emergence of the strictly "biblical" type of preaching in our own day is that many have felt that the efforts of the nineteenth and early twentieth centuries to translate had only succeeded in betraying. In some instances this may have been the case. But the modern cure seems often to be worse than the old disease. For what is nowadays preached by those who follow the new and fashionable school is frequently simply unintelligible, meaningless, without significance, to a very considerable proportion of their hearers, both those who are within the

Church itself and even more those who are outside the "blessed company of faithful people."

Christian thinkers must necessarily be engaged in the "reconception" of the faith of the Church. During the past half-century there were men like William Sanday and James Franklin Bethune-Baker and William Porcher DuBose, to name only Anglicans—and there were many others in other Christian bodies. These men were not "reductionists," in the sense that they were seeking to lower the claims of the gospel. Neither were they "minimizers," in the sense that they were willing to make the Christian faith an easy and simple thing which would appeal to any "man of good will." On the contrary, they were intent on taking the essential core of Christianity, which is the gospel of the living God, the proclamation of God's presence and work in Christ for men's wholeness, and on so thinking it through again, so "re-conceiving" its implications, so teaching it and so preaching it, that people living in their own time could *hear* it and, if they were willing to make the commitment and surrender, accept it for themselves.

In the past few decades we have had a great theological revival. Some of its contributions have been of enormous value to us all, but many of them seem to be both dangerous and unfortunate. For the over-all result of the great reaction has been a sophistication of the true simplicity of the gospel, the use of a jargon which the common man (and the intelligent one, too, often enough) cannot understand, and a tendency to assume that the biblical and creedal language *as it stands* need only be spoken, and enough then has been done to state and communicate the point of the Christian proclamation. Yet the early Church itself, when it departed from biblical idiom at the Council of Nicea and used for theological purposes a non-biblical word, *homo-ousion,* as the guarantor of true biblical meaning, gave Christians in later days a charter for translation—provided always that it is the gospel, its setting and its significance, that we are translating, and not some bright and novel ideas of our own.

Surely I need not labor the point. No preacher with any sensitivity can do other than agree that he does not easily "get the message across." Nor would he claim, if he is honest with himself and about those to whom he speaks, that it is the sinfulness of his hearers, and that alone, which gets in his way. He would say that to a considerable degree it is just that he is not understood. And he would admit that he is not understood because he is talking in patterns which have little or no point of contact with those who listen. His statement of the gospel is couched too often in language and in a context which bear little or no relationship to the circumstances, the accepted ways of thinking of the world both scientifically and philosophically, in which the hearers live.

Not all of these circumstances, these accepted ways of thinking, are wicked and wrong. That would be an easy way out of our problems. We could simply denounce the evil world and leave it there. But God has been speaking in secular ways to men and women through the ages; he has led them into more of the truth about the structure and functioning of the world in which they live; he is at work in the areas of human study, exploration, research, and enquiry, which have given us this "new" world. Doubtless much of what is believed and taught about it is wrong or partially wrong. But in any event this is *where the people live*. This is their *condition.* It is in these terms that they will be reached or they will not be reached at all.

So we need a new kind of approach in our preaching of the gospel; and this approach depends upon a new way of envisaging the gospel itself. On the one hand we dare not attempt to minimize or reduce the historic faith as this centers in the Church's age-old evangel. But on the other hand, we must be willing to take the risk of finding for the gospel new ways of expression which will speak directly and vividly to the hearts of men in this age. One of the corollaries of this attitude and approach will be theological in nature; we shall recognize that there are things central and indispensable, things peripheral and secondary. In fact we shall come to see, as Erasmus once remarked, *quae pertinent ad fidem paucissimis articulis absolvantur*: that the things which pertain to the faith are to be phrased in as few articles as possible.

What is needed is to see that we do not seek a "new thing," but we do seek to preach the old gospel in a "new way." I am here paraphrasing Vincent of Lerins' great phrase, *non nova sed nove*. The gospel which we preach is the Church's gospel and we preach it in the context of the life of the Church. The gospel is the very meaning of the Church's existence; it *is* the Church's existence. It—or rather, he who is its heart—is the *raison d'être* of "the Holy Church throughout the world." If the Church did not have this gospel, it would be simply a more or less interesting sociological phenomenon. Because it has this gospel, it is the community of faith in which men respond to him whom the gospel proclaims: Jesus Christ the Lord as God's definitive and focal action for man's wholeness. But the converse is also true.

The gospel without the Church would be the gospel without a setting and therefore a barren and sterile thing. Preachers of the gospel would be voices "crying in the wilderness." We who are preachers of the gospel are also ministers of the Church, administrators of the sacraments; we are ministers of *Christ* in his Church and we are ministers of the *Church* of Christ.

2.

THE

SETTING

OF THE

GOSPEL

As those who have been ordained to the ministry in the Church of Christ, it is our duty to be "faithful dispensers of the Word of God and of his holy Sacraments." And we are to do this in the Church.

So it is that in the fulfillment of our task of preaching the gospel, we are to proclaim it in the setting and in the context of the life of "the blessed company of all faithful people." We are not commissioned to preach our own private "gospel"; we are not to proclaim some message which we have ourselves discovered; we are not to expound to our hearers some fancy, however brilliant, that has occurred to our own enlightened spirits. As ministers, we are "men under authority"—the authority of Christ our Lord, certainly, but the authority of our Lord as he has given it to us in and through and by his Body, the Church. This is the common teaching of all Christian bodies; this is "ecumenical doctrine" if ever there be such a thing.

Of course, when I say that we are "to preach in the Church," I am not referring to the church building; for much of our preaching may very well be outside that building. When John Wesley travelled all over England, declaring the gospel of Christ in the fields and on the village commons, in the streets of large towns and in public places in the country-side, he was still acting as an ordained minister of the Church and he was still preaching *in* the Church—although the authorities of the Established Church of England, regrettably, did not seem willing to recognize what should have been a patent and wonderful fact. To preach "in the Church" is to preach by and through our belonging to the Church; it is to preach because we are the Church's ministers, ordained for this very purpose and with the authority and commissioning which the Church gives for speaking and acting in its name. The life of the Church, its worship, its very existence as the "people of God," is the setting for our proclamation of the *kerygma*.

But there is even more than this to be said. For the Church is not only the setting for our *preaching* of the gospel; it is also, in a very profound sense, the setting for the gospel *itself*. Professor John Knox has urged in his many books, and with that simplicity of utterance, persuasiveness of argument, and depth of Christian understanding that we have come to expect from him, that in the total Christian "thing," so to say, there is more than one essential element. He has demonstrated that in the "event of Christ," we have, of course, the historical person who was born, who lived and taught, who died and was known again as risen from the dead; but there was also the context into which Jesus came, a situation which had been made ready to receive him. The older Israel, "Israel after the flesh," as we may say, was necessarily part of the total reality; without it his historical appearance would have been as it were a "flash in the pan." And there was another element too, especially necessary; there was the Christian community, compounded (as Professor Knox himself has shown us in his notable book *The Early Church and the Coming Great Church*) of "memory" and "the Spirit," remembering the Lord and living in the new energy which his coming had released into the world. Had there been no community, springing into being in consequence of the person of Jesus as he met the response of his hearers and his followers, the Christian gospel could not have been communicated; indeed, it could not have existed, for the gospel exists precisely in the action of God in Christ as this action is received, apprehended, realized, known, shared, and lived by the children of God to whom in his love he reveals himself.

Thus the Church is not an incidental appendage to the Word of God; it is not an accidental accompaniment of the Christian faith. It is in itself a part of the gospel of the living God as Christians know and cherish that gospel. The Church is part of the gospel because it is the community of those who, in responding to God's love in Jesus Christ, have found themselves knit together in a fellowship which both "remembers" him who brought it into being and which also is possessed by his Spirit and instinct with his life. Thus it is in the Church that Jesus Christ is a present reality, known to his people; and being known in this manner, he is preached by the Church as the Lord. St. Paul may have spoken of "my gospel," but not for a moment did he intend or imply that it was his in any personal possessive sense; it was *his,* rather, because it was the gospel which he as a person had preached and was still preaching. It was the *true* gospel as over against the distortions and the deviations which he saw elsewhere. It was *his as the true* gospel because he was himself a man "in Christ"—and that phrase signified for him, as his letters make abundantly clear, that he was, and knew himself to be, what the Book of Common Prayer calls—in another phrase which yet is remarkably Pauline in expression—"a very member incorporate in the mystical Body of Christ, which is the blessed company of all faithful people."

So it is with each one of us who is ordained. We are ordained to the ministry of the Church—the "sacred ministry," as it is called; but that ordination of ours does not give us any personal rights or privileges which come to us through some peculiar claim of our own. In Anglican theology, for example, the high doctrine of the ministry, such as was taught by the great Oxford divine of the last century, R. C. Moberly, in his notable book *Ministerial Priesthood,* is intent on making quite clear that there can be no separation of the Church's ordained minister from the life of the Church. On the contrary, Moberly is emphatic in his insistence that the ordained minister functions only in and as a "ministerial agent" of the Church's priesthood and ministry. Moberly argues that it is only against the background of the royal priesthood which is Christ's own, and which Christ wills to share with his Church, and in the context of the priesthood of the laity or the "people of God," a priesthood which belongs to "every member of the same in his vocation and ministry," that "priesthood" can be ascribed to the ordained ministry at all.

In different ways and with differing emphasis all Christian communions—even, in certain respects, the Roman Catholic Church, at least in its best theologians like St. Thomas Aquinas—say much the same thing. It is not without significance that this is so; and it is not without importance, either, for the eventual reconciliation of Christian bodies in one visible Catholic Church—although this is a point which has only recently been brought to the fore and given the emphasis it deserves in ecumenical discussion.

Thus there is no unbridgeable chasm between laity and ministry, between "priest" and "people." All of us, clergy and nonclergy, are members together in the *laos tou theou,* the "people of God"; and all of us share in the derivative priesthood which is given to the Church from and through and in Christ its Lord and Head. To be ordained to the specific office of ministry is indeed to be given a specific function in the Church; and some of us would add that this ordination includes a *character* in the theological sense of the term —that is, it includes a particular *stamp* given to the ordained minister as a man approved by the Church and in it chosen by God to act for the people of God and to serve ministerially in the fellowship from God to the people. But even so, this fact is never understood as setting a man "off" from, even though it does give him a special role within, the total life of the Church of Christ.

This theological statement has to be made if we are to draw certain practical conclusions of great importance. Those conclusions, indeed, are not in and of themselves particularly novel; yet without a theological setting they are liable to much misunderstanding.

The first of the practical conclusions has to do with the

tremendous responsibility laid on the minister always to speak and act for, and in, and of, the Church of Christ in which he has been ordained a minister. Here we are referring, not to any specific denomination or sect, any one communion of Christians but to the Church of God in its whole catholic reality. It is the Church's gospel we are to proclaim; it is not our own particular message which happens to appeal to our own particular tastes. But there is an opposite, and equally important, truth. To preach with this sense of responsibility does not mean, and must not mean, that we are to preach in a fashion which we might style "automatic." Sometimes we hear sermons marked by an almost indefinable "official" quality; we hear the kind of preaching in which the minister's personal apprehension of the gospel is forgotten in the official nature of his office as preacher. Sometimes it is assumed that the preacher, precisely because he is the proclaimer of the Church's gospel and not of some gospel of his own creation, must as a preacher be something other than a fully personal human being with his own personal understanding of the gospel, his own personal interpretation of it, and his own personal way of expressing it. Sometimes one is horrified at the way in which some of the younger disciples of the various neo-orthodox and neo-catholic movements—I say "movements," in the plural, for there seem to be several of them—act in this fashion and defend their wooden and "official" preaching on the ground that they must in no way obtrude their personalities between the gospel and the hearers. Of course the result is that they obtrude their personalities much more obnoxiously than if they preached simply and naturally. No man can be completely "official," try as hard as he may, for no man can contract out of his humanity at will; and a proper recognition of our responsibility in preaching for and in the Church does not mean that we try to be other than ourselves. To be human *means* to be *a* person, with one's own particular qualities, characteristics, ways of seeing and saying things. The wonderful truth is that God will accept all these, once we put them at his disposal; he will use them to make the gospel *of the Church*, as each of us apprehends it, effective to those who listen. The very fact that it is *we* who are speaking has its own added significance, for it indicates something of the wonderful richness of the gospel by which the Church lives.

We are obliged, as Christians, to be ourselves; we can never be anybody else, anyway; and as the Church's men we are not less men—despite the nasty little remark that there are three sexes, men and women and clergymen. If we are *ourselves,* as God means us to be and as the Church would have us to be, then necessarily we are men living at a given time, in a given place, under given conditions, with given ways of seeing and doing. That is the meaning of humanity, with the historical conditioning which is proper to humankind. In consequence, we preach as *ourselves*—we preach, that is, as modern men and women who yet believe the gospel and who have been commissioned by the Church to preach it. In consequence, each of us is given the obligation to think his way into and make his own the Christian tradition as a whole; each of us must seek to penetrate for himself into the deep meaning of the *kerygma* which is the heart of the tradition; each of us must make it his own in his own idiom. It is peculiarly the task of the clergy to do this, for they have—or should see to it that peripheral activities do not prevent their having—both the learning and (dare I say it?) the time for the job as the laity do not have.

A second practical consequence of the truth that the Church is the setting for the gospel of God in Jesus Christ is that we preach to make men members of the Church. The gospel is the Church's gospel. It is the gospel which gives its *raison d'être* to the Church, but there is a deep sense in which, as we have seen, one must say that the Church also gives its *raison d'être* to the gospel. Not, of course, that the Church created the gospel out of its own fancy or desire or idealizing tendency. The Word of God is *there*; the Word of God incarnate in Jesus Christ is the given *prius* for the Church. In Professor Knox's terminology, the *person* of Christ has a certain kind of priority in the total *event* of Christ. But yet it is the purpose of God to incorporate men into a new community, to lift them to what might be styled a new level of "human being," to make them men "in Christ" —and all this as they respond in faith, love, and service, to the gospel of his Son. To be "in Christ" is in New Testament thought to be "in the Church," to belong to the family of God in Christ, to share together in the common life which the Lord who is proclaimed in the gospel opens up for those whom he did not refuse to call his brethren.

Dr. R. Douglas Richardson, sometime principal of Ripon Hall in Oxford, has put this in telling words: "The volume of life that flows from Jesus Christ is the greatest experience that men have ever had: 'the Life, the Eternal Life which was with the Father,' as the writer of I John says, has through him welled up in millions until they have felt their life to be taken up into him." This means, Dr. Richardson points out, that "so deeply is Christianity derived from the person of Christ that it has been said that Christianity *is* Christ." Precisely: "for me to live *is* Christ," St. Paul wrote; and for the Apostle, as for every other Christian, the very life which as a Christian he lives, in fellowship with God in Christ and in fellowship with the brethren through that "exchange" which is the secret of Christian discipleship, is both the life of Christ himself and the life of the Church of Christ. St. Augustine wrote of *Christus caput et corpus*: Christ head and body, as the one Christ who now lives forevermore; and the Epistle to the Ephesians, as Dr. J. Armitage Robinson noted many years ago, is a long meditation on the theme that the Christian is not to think of Christ *and* his followers so much as of Christ *in his members*. The Lord, who is proclaimed in the gospel as God's definitive and focal activity in manhood for our wholeness, takes us into himself, makes us one with himself, lives in us as we live in him, to the end that we may be knit together in "a bundle of life" in a much deeper sense than the Old Testament writer of that wonderful phrase could ever understand. The Church, then, is itself part of the gospel we preach; it came into being in and round and through response to him who is the subject of the gospel; it exists to witness to and keep the gospel; it is the setting in which the gospel is preached and heard and appropriated and made a vital and vitalizing reality in the experience of those who are brought to the Church's Lord.

One of the most important developments in the Christian world in our day is an awakened sense of the Church as the *una sancta,* the one holy people of the one holy God as he has manifested himself in his incarnate Son. The very essence of the ecumenical movement is in this new awareness; it recognizes that only through an ever-deepening understanding of this truth and its centrality in Christian life can Christian reunion become a living possibility. Through a renewed study of the biblical record and witness, as well as through the pressure of events in our time, men and women of all Christian groups are coming more and more to see that the Church is no afterthought; it is bound up with the fact of Christian faith and the faith in the Christian fact.

In the New Testament the Church is seen as the new and true Israel of God. The older Israel, chosen as the Jews believed to be God's very people, had rejected the promised Messiah when he came; but the "little flock," and those who responded to their preaching, had remained faithful, had accepted the Messiah; and now, round him risen from the dead, they were constituted the new "chosen people," "called of God," the *ekklesia kyriake,* called according to promise and given responsibilities commensurate with that calling. So the Church is the "new covenant," the "new testament in Christ's blood"; and into it are to be brought all those, whether Greek or Jew, barbarian or Scythian, male or female, bond or free, who will answer the preaching of the Church by a surrender of themselves to the Lord who is the living head of the new community.

Our preaching of the gospel is a carrying out of this responsibility which has been laid upon the Church. The Church is preaching through us: Christ our Lord in his Church is calling men through our preaching. This is our share in the ministry of reconciliation: that "God in Christ was reconciling the world unto himself and has committed unto us the word of reconciliation." We preach in the setting of the Church, that men may be reconciled to God. And the reconciliation is made effectual when those who respond to its proclamation are incorporated into the life which has been opened up for them: the life "in Christ" which is the fellowship of the Holy Spirit, the living Church. So all preaching is set in the context of the Church's worship and devotion, as well as of the Church's shepherding and serving of God's children.

When the gospel was preached by the primitive Church, it was preached with expectation of a result. Since God had done, was doing, and would do, such and such things, *now therefore repent* and be baptized. Repentance, a change of orientation, a "new look," was expected as the result of the preaching; and in consequence of that repentance, men would seek entrance into the Christian community. They would be baptized. Initiation into the life of the Christian fellowship was the hoped-for effect of the proclamation of the Word.

That at once suggests an aspect of preaching which today needs the strongest emphasis. For those who are outside the Church, for the pagans and for the "god-fearers" of our time, we are to preach to the end that they shall repent and seek entrance into the fellowship of Christ through baptism. This is why it is so very important that we should not confine our preaching to those who are already of our Christian company. It is our task, as it is our bounden duty, to find ways in which we may bring the message of the gospel to those who are outside the Church. It is not my intention to discuss such ways of reaching the "unchurched"; suffice it to say that the World Council of Churches has lately been studying the problem of evangelism and has recognized that the older methods, effective enough in their time, will not serve today and new methods need to be found. Even such organizations as the "service clubs," so often regarded with contempt by the self-righteous, should be used as means for reaching those with whom otherwise we do not readily come into contact—not to speak of the use of labor chaplaincies, industrial chaplaincies, and many other agencies and devices.

For those who are already within the Church, entered on our lists as baptized (and in Anglican circles "confirmed") communicants, we have a responsibility too. Is our preaching such as shall strengthen them in their church-belonging, deepen in them their apprehension of the Church's gospel, enable them to appropriate more fully the grace of God in Christ as this is known and shared in the fellowship? These persons are already members of the Church; many of them are already communicants. But certainly it ought to be clear that our preaching must have as one of its aims what we might describe as the consolidation of their belonging.

In all of our preaching, we are not talking in the air, giving voice to speculations and theories; we are not handing out a set of theological opinions for discussion by our hearers. We are preaching, always and ever, "for decisions." In fact, we are doing every Sunday what Dr. Billy Graham says is his constant purpose. Whatever we may think of Dr. Graham's own preaching, and the content of it, he is right at least in this respect. "For decisions"—which means that when we preach Christ as "the way, the truth, and the life," as God's definitive and focal action for man's wholeness, we are preaching not that men and women may "accept Christ," as it were, in a vacuum, but that they may be *of his flock,* in his Church. Or if they are already in it through present membership, we are preaching with the purpose that they may grow in the knowledge and love of Christ, the Church's Lord, more fully appropriate his grace in the community of his people, and more profoundly realize what it means to be incorporated into his ongoing life in the fellowship of the Church.

They who are commissioned to preach the gospel are preaching, then, in order that men will respond in faith and will grow in Christ's knowledge and love, becoming participant in his very life. Among other things, and central among them, this means, for all of us who are historical Christians, that such men will become devout, faithful, penitent, and regular communicants at the sacrament of the Lord's Supper.

It has been said over and over again, by Christians of all kinds in this mainstream of historic Christianity, that the Eucharist, the Holy Communion, the Lord's Supper, the Liturgy, the Divine Mysteries, the Mass—call it what you will—is the Church's characteristic action. Here the Church is doing what it ought to be doing. Now if that be true, then the Eucharist is also the characteristic action of every Christian. For it is in the Lord's Supper that the gospel comes alive in a very special way. The sacramental action of the Church in celebrating the Eucharist is the living enactment of the gospel which is proclaimed by preaching; Luther was insistent on the point that the gospel is enacted in the sacrament, and he was altogether right in this insistence. Hence our preaching of the gospel should lead men to the Holy Table, to the altar if we may use that word, where the Word which we proclaim becomes, through God's gracious action of blessing and giving, the Word which is "received by faith with thanksgiving." Whatever may be our eucharistic theology, the fact remains that the Holy Communion is the distinctively Christian act of worship and that regularity in attending and receiving it is expected of every Christian who understands his discipleship.

When I was a boy, my parish priest used to say that he preached for "more communions." If he had meant by this that he wanted merely a numerical increase, larger figures in a statistical summary, he was saying something that was neither right nor Christian. But he did not mean that. What he meant was that he preached so that his people would more regularly, more devoutly, more penitently, more faithfully, frequent the Lord's Table. He was profoundly evangelical in the very best sense of the word. Indeed it is here that preaching can be of special importance. All too often Christians of whatever description have a tendency to turn the sacrament into an almost magical rite, by reason of their failure to understand quite clearly that "faith is the means whereby we receive" it. On the other hand, all too often Christians have managed to make the sacrament an occasional appendage to what is in fact a nonsacramental Christianity, by reason of their failure to grasp the great truth that it is "the gospel in action," as well as by reason of their failure to demand and make use of frequent occasions for its celebration. Hence preaching of the gospel should have as one of its main objectives the preparation of our people for the faithful receiving of the "sacrament of the body and blood of Christ," "to their great and endless comfort," and in consequence of this, a strong desire on their part for more frequent opportunities to receive it. If we grasp this aspect of our preaching, we may well have our part in a great move-

ment of return to the intention of the Reformers of the sixteenth century as well as of the Fathers of the ancient
Church: that the Lord's Supper shall in very deed be the act
of Christian worship most loved, most used, and most hon-
ored by the whole of the Christian world, without base super-
stition or ungodly fear but in loving obedience to the command of the Lord and for the "strengthening and refresh-
ing" of his people.

Normal Sunday Christian worship, we are more and more
coming to recognize, should be a service in which the Word
is preached *and* the sacrament received. This is what the
ancient Church did; this is what the Reformers intended and
desired; this is what the remarkable "liturgical revival" in
our day, found as it is in all Christian churches, seeks to restore. The regular Sunday-by-Sunday spiritual "diet" of
every Christian should be one act of worship in which the two
elements of sermon and sacrament are combined. It is not
the fault of our Reformers, whether on the continent of
Europe or in England, that this has not been the case; it has
been the laziness, the lack of interest, the spiritual indifference or poverty, of the people which has prevented its realization; and a large measure of the blame for these things
must fall on the shoulders of the ministers of God's Word and
sacraments. It has been an almost unmitigated tragedy that
the regular preaching of the gospel has been separated so
often from the sacrament, and the celebration of the sacrament from the preaching of the gospel; the awful truth is
that both have suffered from the separation and the encouraging fact is that both will benefit enormously by a return by
us all to the norm of Christian worship.

Anglicans have a special opportunity today to work

towards the strengthening of the already active movement for the establishment each Sunday of a Parish Communion, held at a convenient hour when men and women can come together as a congregation to hear the Word proclaimed and to receive the sacramentally communicated life of the Lord about whom the Word speaks. We must repent of the misunderstanding of the real meaning of worship which led the Oxford Movement and its successors to emphasize "early celebration for communion" and "late celebration for worship and preaching"; just as we must also repent of the equally sad misunderstanding which led others to substitute Morning Prayer for the Holy Communion as a normal Sunday morning act of worship. In other Christian communions there is also need for repentance, and for a recovery of the norm in worship; and one of the encouraging signs of the times is the increasing frequency of celebrations of the Lord's Supper in all denominations and the increasing emphasis which is being laid on its central place in the Christian life. This has nothing whatever to do with "party" allegiance in any given church, nor with the differences, such as they are, between Anglicans and Presbyterians or Lutherans or Congregationalists or Methodists or any other Christians. It is simply and solely a matter of the integrity of the Christian Church and the fullness of the Christian life.

The Church of Christ, which is the setting for the gospel and for the preaching of the gospel, is something other than the given empirical Christian bodies with their membership lists—or perhaps it would be better to say that Christ's Church is not *other than* but *more than* those bodies, either taken separately or taken as a group. The Church of Christ is *Christ's* Church; it is the *una sancta,* as our continental brethren like to say; it is, in the words of the *Te Deum,* "the holy Church throughout all the world," and it is also the Church "in heaven," including those who have gone from our sight in this world but who are still with Christ and are sharers in his grace. There is nothing more presumptuous nor less fruitful in this connection, than to try to fix the limits of that Church which is Christ's Church. "The Lord knows who are his"; and so far as we are concerned, we get out of any definition of the limits of the Church exactly as much as we put into that definition.

There is no Christian communion which does not have some theological device for getting into the Church in the widest sense those who are not, so to say, "officially" included in some particular definition. Traditional Catholicism speaks of baptism by blood, by intention, by desire; and some of the great Catholic doctors have even spoken of every soul which loves truth as being somehow part of the Church whose Lord is himself the Truth. The Reformed communions have had the conception of "uncovenanted grace," to bring in those who seem to be outside the "covenant"; or they have talked about the "latent" Church as well as the "patent" Church; or they have made a contrast between the Church "invisible" as known to God alone and the Church "visible" here in earth. Surely all of this points in one direction. It is impossible for men to tell God what he shall do or to set limits to his grace and mercy. On the other hand, however, it has been a deep and abiding instinct of all Christians to see that without fellowship with others who belong to Christ there can really be no "salvation" at all, no wholeness of life such as comes from living in the community of the brethren who like ourselves have been made brothers of the living Lord.

Whatever St. Cyprian may have meant by his dictum *extra ecclesiam nulla salus,* it cannot mean for us that outside the *empirical* Church as it is known and visible on earth, there is no possibility of the redeemed life with God in Christ. An Eastern Orthodox priest once remarked in my hearing that the real meaning of the Cyprianic phrase must be that those who are "saved" are saved through the Church, whether or not they recognized or accepted the fact that this was so; but that we dare not, on our side, say just how or when or why this occurred. He spoke with great insight. It is with an exposition of this point and an application of it to the preaching of the Church's gospel that we shall bring this chapter to a close.

If Dr. John Knox is right in his assertion that the response of the community to the "memory" of its Lord and the empowering of that community by the Spirit are integral parts of the total Christian event, two things would seem to follow. The first point to be noted is that in order for Christianity *to be* Christianity at all there must be the Church. In this sense Christology and ecclesiology are almost one and the same—not that the Church *is* Christ, in a simple way, but that the Church is the indispensable *where* in which Christ is encountered, received, followed. The second point, however, is that the divine Act of self-expression, self-revelation, the raising of men to God in Christ, cannot be *confined* to the historical events which are the origin of our faith. *God is always like that; God is always doing that.*

In terms of Christian theology, this is a way of saying that the Eternal Word, the second hypostasis of the Blessed Trinity, is the eternal Agent of Godhead not only in creation but also in revelation and in restoration. It is a way of saying, too, that while the Eternal Word, the Eternal Christ or Son, is focally manifest in the human life called Jesus, he is not *confined* to that life. Rather, he is *defined by it*. And wherever response is made to him—response which is in reality nothing but response in and by the Holy Spirit, who in the Godhead *is* Response, or as Emil Brunner has so nobly put it, "the Amen" in God—there those who respond have been caught up into a fellowship which in the most profound way (even if not visible) *is* the life of the true and abiding Church, "without spot or wrinkle, or any such thing." So the Church in this highest and most wonderful sense is indeed a "sacred mystery," as the ancient Gelasian collect puts it. As the Church, known to us empirically, is the setting and context of the gospel historically understood by us, so the Church, as God's own mystery, is the setting and context for the gospel in its eternal and cosmic range and sweep.

No preacher should think this too "mystical"; in truth it is the factor which saves his preaching from triviality, parochialism, mere "this-world-ism," and gives to our faith in the Lord of the gospel a glorious and illimitable quality. It is against that vastly extended background in the light of those vistas of eternity, that we can preach *this* decisive action in the Man Jesus. So we can make our own the words of a noble Latin hymn of the ninth century:

> Only-begotten, Word of God eternal,
> Lord of creation, merciful and mighty,
> Hear now thy servants, when their joyful voices
> > Rise to thy presence.

Yes, it is in that setting, in that context, that the Word of God is to be proclaimed. For the gospel of God in Christ is the explanation of what thus "goes on" in the Church, as it is the proclamation of the Church's very existence in Christ. The end of it all is that, incorporated into him and sharing in the fellowship of all the faithful, whoever they may be, known or unknown to us, we may come to sing with that ancient hymn-writer his paean of praise:

> God in three Persons, Father everlasting,
> Son co-eternal, ever-blessed Spirit,
> Thine be the glory, praise, and adoration
>   Now and for ever.

3.

THE PEOPLE
TO WHOM
WE
PREACH

Some years ago Dr. Thoedore Parker Ferris, rector of Trinity Church in Boston, in discussing the problem of preaching in the contemporary situation, described the preacher's task as that of "bringing the *given* gospel to the *given* world"— and particularly to men and women to whom we preach here and now, where we have been placed by God in this world of the mid-twentieth century. For there can be no question that we do preach to that "given" world and to the men and women in it. Whether we like it or not, we preach to them as they really are in concrete fact; we do not preach to some fanciful group of people living in an imagined situation which may happen to appeal to us. If the gospel which we are commissioned to preach is "given" to us, so is the world in which we preach it and the people to whom we preach it. There is no escape possible for us.

First, something should be said about "given-ness" and its profound religious implications. One of the great spiritual writers of the French Roman Catholic Church was Jean de Caussade, whose writings have been made known to us through Miss Evelyn Underhill. Nothing which that master of spirituality wrote or said is so important as his insistence, found over and over again in his letters and his essays in "spiritual direction," that it is the "present moment," the exact place where we are, the time in which we live, the situation in our existence is set, which constitute for us what he liked to call the "sacrament" of God's presence with us. That situation, that moment, that "given" time and place, provide, he said, the location and the occasion in which, and in which alone, we are able to meet and know God; and de Caussade maintained that any attempt on our part to evade that situation, to run away from it, to seek for God somewhere else, is bound to lead us astray. This truth needs emphasizing in our own religious life; and for the preacher its application is of supreme importance. For surely the preacher of the gospel is to declare the Word of God in the place where the preacher is, to the people whom he has before him, and with the most humble and honest recognition that that place and those people are "given" him by God and that he must keep that "given-ness" constantly in his thinking and speaking. If he tries to escape this, then he is "running away"—and he is running away not only from his ministerial duty and his ministerial privilege, but also from God himself—for God puts men in the place where they are to serve him; and if they are to serve him at all, they must serve him *there*.

This does not suggest to us, or at least it ought not to suggest, a bovine complacency about the way things are. Obviously it does not mean that there will not be other, and perhaps greater, responsibilities and opportunities for a preacher of the gospel at some other time and in some other place. But what it does mean most certainly, is that for the time being, while he is in *that* place and at *that* time, his duty is to do his work in *that* "given" situation. And the immediate corollary of all this is that the preacher must *know* his people where and as they are. He must know them as they are, not only in those personal matters which any good pastor will appreciate, but also in their patterns of thought, in the ideas they have, in the notions they accept, in the "facts of life" as they see them, and with the needs that they feel. Dr. Ferris's "given world" is, then, the world of the twentieth century in which we are living; and the people who live along with us live in it, are the people to whom we are to proclaim the gospel.

In that sense, every one will admit that we must be "up to date." This does not mean that we should have a "nice modern gospel," which is specially tailored to meet the requirements of our less exacting contemporaries. We cannot cut the gospel to "what Jones likes." But when we preach the real gospel, the Church's gospel, the historic gospel, we need to remember always that we preach it to people who are real people, who are our own contemporaries. For it is they to whom we are sent. In preaching to them we are not only fulfilling our proper responsibility as ministers of Christ's Church, but are also serving and meeting God in the concrete situation in which, by his grace, we have been placed.

Now, what sort of people are these to whom we speak?

What sort of world is it in which they live? What are their ways of seeing and understanding things?

First of all, there is the prevalence in the contemporary world of what is usually called "the scientific outlook" or "the scientific attitude." There can be no doubt that a dominant motif in the cultural pattern of our time is the high respect which is felt for science and the tremendous attention and respect which are paid to its supposed findings. It is not so much that the special results in this or that field are known in detail to our people; rather, the point is that their way of seeing and thinking is molded to an enormous degree by the outlook or attitude which in the widest sense may be styled "scientific."

Professor C. A. Coulson, a distinguished Oxford mathematician and physicist, has recently given an admirable description of this attitude as it manifests itself in modern life. Science, he tells us, is for vast numbers of people

the sure and safe ground on which to build a way of life. . . . This conviction about science lies deep in the subconscious thinking of the ordinary man, who sees all around him the exciting and varied products of a technology that provides for almost every physical and mental need, and who concludes that the scientific mode of thought and experiment out of which this technology grew is large enough, and solid enough, to be a chief foundation for his life.

Professor Coulson is himself a devout English Methodist; but he is honest enough to see facts for what they are. He goes on to quote some words from a former president of the Carnegie Endowment for International Peace:

The greatest event in the world today is not the awakening of Asia nor the rise of communism—vast and portentous as these events are. It is the advent of a new way of living, due to science, a change in the conditions of the world and the structure of society which began not so very long ago in the West and is now reaching out over all mankind.

He quotes further, this time from a distinguished scientist: "At the present time only science has the vigour and the authority of achievement, to make . . . the highest human values captivate men's hearts and minds, and restore faith in them." All this is from Professor Coulson's essay in the symposium *An Approach to Christian Education*. The professor himself does not agree with the judgment that only science can do these things; he believes that religious faith, and above all Christian faith, must somehow be restored to men and women today. But he indicates one of the most significant aspects of our contemporary scene and one with which preachers of the gospel necessarily have to deal if they are to bring that gospel home to their hearers.

What Dr. Coulson has noted has been put for us in another way by Dr. Derwyn Owen, Provost of Trinity College, Toronto, in his excellent study of the present "cult" of science, entitled *Scientism, Man, and Religion*. Dr. Owen describes the modern and widespread phenomenon of "scientolatry" (as he styles it) as including five basic assumptions which help to make up the scientific outlook or attitude which is generally accepted among our contemporaries. Here are the five, in Dr. Owen's listing: (1) truth is available through science alone; (2) matter is the primary reality; (3) all behavior is determined; (4) all values are social conventions and hence are "relative" rather than absolute in significance; (5) the coming of an ideal society is guaranteed through science. I am not so sure that the fifth of these is as widespread as Dr. Owen thinks, although he makes a very good case for it; but no sensitive observer of our age can deny that the other four come very close to "hitting the mark." The extraordinary thing is that even among our own people, such assumptions are often held, albeit quite unconsciously.

The point to be stressed is that science and scientific ways of thinking are so widely accepted that for vast numbers of people—and not only for those who are described as being "educated," but also by some sort of cultural "osmosis" for the rest of the population—these ideas are often simply taken for granted. They form part of the mental furniture; they are simply there, unquestioned even if not explicitly and consciously held. And it is apparent that for such persons, religion is bound to seem to belong to the realm of the "merely ideal," some vague area which does not actually get anything done. This is why we hear so much about "religion" as a way in which moral character is promoted and some sense of peace and security engendered. But the *gospel,* in its terrible reality, is very hard for such people to understand, much less to accept.

We might at this point examine these assumptions, consider this attitude or outlook, and demonstrate its utter inadequacy, not only in respect to its philosophical implications but in its consequences in practical experience, but all this has been done admirably by Dr. Owen himself, as well as by Professor Coulson. In fact it is part of the stock-in-trade of most contemporary writing in defense of Christian faith. What we must say emphatically, however, is that we shall never get very far in our preaching if we spend our time ignorantly sneering at science, impatiently rejecting its attitude or outlook *in toto,* or pretending to do this—for I doubt if we could manage to do it completely. There is really no use in turning our sermons into demonstrations that insofar as science is thus understood and portrayed it is a "false Messiah." Of course it is a "false Messiah"; we all know that. But it is highly important for us to realize that with whatever modifications may be required in the interests of honesty and accuracy, not to say modesty in its claims, the scientific attitude in its broader sense is *here to stay.* The scientific way of seeing things, of handling things, of acting upon things, is going to continue to be one of the ways in which men and women will look at their world and at themselves. We cannot *wish* it away; we must find a place for it in the total Christian view. We cannot claim that it is irrelevant; we must claim that it is revelatory—revelatory of God and his ways in his world.

My first suggestion is that we should not waste time by pretending to show that the scientific attitude is *all wrong.* It is our task to show, with all the wit and wisdom we can summon, that it is not *enough.* This attitude, so widespread today, may be true so far as it goes, but it is not adequate to the whole of human life, to the entire human situation, to the total world in which we live. The way to show this is not by making snide attacks on science but by the continuing demonstration that the greatest things about life, as every man knows them, are never exhaustively stated in a scientific formula and never exhaustively described in a scientific picture. If a personal experience may be cited, I myself had an illustration of the success of this method not long ago, when I had the privilege of preaching for several days to a large university audience. It occurred to me that I might show that no student would willingly "exhaust" the "meaning" of his fiancée in the terms of physics or chemistry or biology or psychology or sociology. In this way the group was brought to the place where the specific claims made in the gospel for God's personal relationship with men could at least be *heard,* even it they were not accepted. I am sure that I should have got nowhere at all if I had turned those sermons into denunciations of science or a contemptuous dismissal of what most of the young people present simply took for granted; they would have rejected the whole thing and stopped listening.

In the second place, it is essential that we take every opportunity to make it perfectly clear that the Christian gospel is not bound up with out-of-date scientific ideas. Most of us take that for granted and assume that our hearers take it for granted, too. But this is a highly unrealistic attitude. For we are not yet far enough away from the days of the Tennessee "trial" of a schoolteacher over the teaching of biological evolution to take it for granted that everybody understands perfectly well that "science" and "religion" are in no essential conflict. Yet the clergy do make this assumption all too often. University students especially need assurance on this matter. Even among quite intelligent men and women, there are many today who do not understand that scientific methods and religious experience can dwell together; they still wonder about the relation of divine creation and natural evolution; they are still very doubtful as to the possibility of their holding to religious convictions and at the same time honestly accepting the findings of the laboratory. Far too many preachers are simply not realistic about the situation. They tend to think the problem has been solved for every body when in fact even they themselves may only have shelved it.

The problem is compounded for us by the reappearance in recent years of biblical fundamentalism. A relatively small number of earnest Christians, frightened by the "risk" which comes from taking scientific biblical studies seriously and above all afraid of the honest attempt to bring scientific understanding and biblical thought into some kind of unity, have retreated into a theological "never-never land" where they may talk among themselves about the religion they hold without exposing it to the attacks of modern scientific thinking. They produce spokesmen who are extremely vocal, although not very enlightened; and the end-result of it all is that the word gets around that this *is* Christianity and that the gospel, if it is to be accepted at all, must be understood in this way. Of course the number of those who respond to biblical fundamentalism is relatively small, but it is just large enough to make the report seem probable— and in consequence, a surprisingly large number of men and women who might be reached by a more intelligent presentation are "put off" Christianity once for all. In circles where biblical fundamentalism is impossible, we often find its partner-in-arms, creedal and ecclesiastical fundamentalism. Here certain articles of the historic creeds, or certain statements in the Reformation confessions of faith, or certain inherited structures in the ecclesiastical body, are set off from all critical examination in the same fashion as that which is found in the biblicist's treatment of the Bible. But once again, this narrow interpretation leads many others to identify the Christian gospel with what seems to them an impossible obscurantism.

In contrast to all this, our task is to speak in such a fashion that the ordinary man or woman can see that they can quite well be "scientifically minded," as they might put it, open to new knowledge from any and every realm, but that at the same time, with complete honesty and integrity, they can hold to the affirmations of faith which the preaching of the Church's gospel is concerned to evoke in them. Yet there is an even deeper problem, one which has to do, not with the specifically scientific attitude or outlook, but with the total pattern of thought in our time.

A quarter of a century ago, in 1932 to be precise, the English philosopher Samuel Alexander addressed the Manchester Science Federation. In the course of his lecture he made a statement which is still worth repeating: "What we need is a religious mythology which is not in complete contradiction of all of our ordinary knowledge." Alexander was a free-thinking but loyal Jew with a deep religious sense, although his philosophical statement of the basis for religion, in his book *Space-Time and Deity,* cannot commend itself to us. He was speaking a long time before the word "myth" became fashionable in theological circles; but what he was saying was, in effect, that the "story" which a religion tells must not be so at variance with the common experience and the accepted patterns of thought of a given age that it seems to the hearers nonsensical or unintelligible. If it does seem nonsensical or unintelligible, the hearers will very likely refuse to give it serious consideration or will reject it out of hand as ridiculously inadequate or totally irrelevant to their actual situation.

It was noteworthy that Alexander did not say that the "religious mythology," to use his own not very satisfactory phrase, must be *identical with* what is taken as "ordinary knowledge." He was not so naïve as to think that a religious interpretation of life, and *a fortiori* the "mythology" upon which religion depends, is simply the republication of such ordinary knowledge, perhaps with the addition of an emotional flavor. He recognized that religion does say *something*; the "myth" brings additional knowledge to us, although in its own way and in its own language, which is not that of scientific or conceptual thinking. So, even in Alexander's terms, we ought not to assume that there is going to be, or should be, a precise correspondence between the common experience and accepted patterns of thought in our or any other age, and the message which is conveyed through the religious story. To put this in another way, the gospel which we preach is not just what everybody believed anyway. A Christian interpretation of life, based on the proclamation that in Christ God is brought near to men for their wholeness, brings into the center of the picture what Professor Tillich has taught us to call our "ultimate concern"; hence it is bound to see all things in a different perspective, to open up to those who accept it wider vistas, and to give such men and women a deeper insight into the meaning of their existence. As a result, it will convince them of the inadequacy, for a full understanding of the meaning of that existence, of the run-of-the-mill experience of men, and of the scientific and philosophical patterns which in any given age seem useful and satisfactory within their proper limits.

On the other hand, however, the Christian interpretation of life need not flatly contradict the best insights, the most thoughtful evaluations and appraisals, and the noblest ideas and aspirations of men in any given culture. It may, indeed it must, *correct* them, especially when they manifest a sinful and stupid pride in man's own unaided and uncriticized abilities and powers; it may, indeed it will, raise to the highest power those aspects of a given culture which do possess truth. What it will *not* do is simply negate such insights, evaluations, appraisals, ideas, and aspirations, and the pattern of culture from which they spring, as if they were sinful in themselves and without any relevance to the religious enterprise.

Alexander's remark has a striking significance for us today, for one of the unfortunate, and indeed highly dangerous, aspects of the present revival of theological interest is precisely the disjunction between the religious "story" and "ordinary knowledge." The particular point to which i should like to direct attention is the contempt now so often manifested in religious circles and in theological discussion for the "reconciliation" of Christian faith with philosophical thought.

This contempt is shown in different ways. With some, it has as its basis a mistaken theological conviction that there can be no "point of contact" between faith and philosophical enquiry. With others, it expresses itself in the notion that religion "has its own logic," which is entirely incommensurable with the common "logic" of other human enterprises. With still others, it is manifested in rather cruder ways, as for example in a glib distinction between "dimensions" of human experience and the assumption that the several dimensions can never meet or intersect. All these attitudes have one thing in common. They seem to have forgotten, if they ever knew, that the demand of men, wherever they may live and whatever they may believe, is always for a real unification of thought and life—a unity in which religious faith may be the highest integrating factor, but a unity which includes within it the rest of human thinking and experience, so that the whole man is at one in his response to the world. These popular contemporary ways of stating the meaning of religion seem to split man up into compartments or to suggest a dizzying variety of quite unrelated ways of adjustment to the world. They might almost be said to glory, of course for what they conceive to be the highest ends, in a kind of schizophrenia.

Again, in sharp contrast to the great tradition of Christian theology, many contemporary religious writers seem to spend most of their time explaining themselves to themselves or their colleagues. They regard theology as the activity by which the Christian thinker articulates or systematizes the experience or life of the Christian community, or creates a schematic summary of the basic data found in the Scriptures upon which the community's life is founded. Professor Alan Richardson, for instance, falls victim to this tendency when he describes theology as the study of the phenomenon presented by the existence of the Christian Church. The whole procedure has a striking resemblance to the way in which, as an old story has it, a band of Chinese shipwrecked on a desert island supported themselves: "they took in each other's laundry."

But in the grand tradition, Christian theology was nothing short of the study of God in relation to everything else. It was not regarded as concerned only with the experience of life in the Christian community, nor solely with the biblical data upon which that community is founded, but with the whole range of life and experience, in every area, as this was related to God. It had to do with God in his relationship to the whole creation; it welcomed as material for its work anything and everything that men had discovered, and it sought to find the divine purpose manifested there; it insisted upon, and gave itself to discover, that basic unity which would give unity to the existence of men. Against this background, the gospel was to be preached. For the Christian gospel made sense of, and gave sense to, this vast mass of data, this enormous range of human experience, which constituted the "ordinary knowledge" of man in the world.

So we are brought back to Alexander's remark. All Christians ought to acknowledge that the "ordinary knowledge" of men, so far as it approximates truth, is the gift of God, who as the divine Reality, is every man's "ultimate concern" and who is inescapably encountered by every man under countless incognitos and through innumerable, and sometimes very strange, media. If that be true, then it is an absolute necessity that our "religious mythology"—the "story" we tell, the gospel we preach—shall be seen to have the most intimate relationship with that knowledge. Our theology, when we come to develop one on the basis of the gospel the Church proclaims, must make sense of and give sense to this knowledge. It is not called to acquiesce without criticism in what people commonly say or think; it must certainly criticize and correct. But at the same time it must be aware of, have respect for, and use this "ordinary knowledge." It must not speak in flat contradiction to it; nor dare it give itself, in its failure to use this "ordinary knowledge," the convenient alibi of claiming that the gospel is necessarily an "offense" and a "scandal."

Of course the gospel is that, but let us be careful about

how we understand what we mean. Alfred North Whitehead once wrote about the "fallacy of the misplaced con-
cretion." We may speak today, in respect of much theological writing and discussion, of the "fallacy of the misplaced
offense." The real offense of the gospel is to sinful, proud,
self-assertive man. As Rudolf Bultmann has rightly remarked, the "offense" or "scandal" ought not to be found
in the sheer irrelevance and utter meaninglessness of the
gospel, when it is interpreted out of all relationship to man's
"ordinary knowledge." To make this vividly clear to contemporary theologians and apologists, and above all to contemporary preachers, is Bultmann's purpose in the contro-
versy which has developed about his ideas; and we should
be able to see this and bring it home to ourselves, without
necessarily adopting Bultmann's own way of meeting the
problem. This is not just a theological issue; it is vital for
the working pastor who is called upon to preach Christ week
by week and day by day. In fact it is he who must be partially concerned. For Sunday by Sunday in his preaching
from the pulpit, and day by day in his pastoral duties which
are nothing but preaching in another manner, he must seek
constantly to bring the "religious mythology" to bear on the
"ordinary knowledge" of the common man.

The pastor of a certain congregation, a man of deep convictions, high ideals, and keen pastoral sense, has succeeded
in nearly emptying his church because, as one of his people,
a devout and dedicated layman, told me, he preaches nothing
but denunciation of all human activity and enterprise as sinful, in contrast to the message of Christ which alone has
value and makes sense. He has failed to give meaning to
and to make meaning of that ordinary experience and gen-

eral knowledge through which, as I firmly believe was recognized by the great doctors of the Christian tradition, God is also speaking and revealing himself to those who hear the gospel.

Surely the proclamation of Jesus Christ, the gospel in its authentic reality, is meant to be the master-light of *all* our seeing; it is meant to enable us to find the presence and purpose of God in *all* our work; it is meant to bring the *whole* world, and every bit of our "ordinary knowledge" about it, into relationship with God in Christ—to the end that finding him and being found of him we may come to live integrated, full, abundant lives, now in this present time and to all eternity. In an age of religious awakening, as many call our day, we must never forget that the gospel is to be preached and taught to people who live with "ordinary knowledge." There is a sense in which insistence on the "relevance" of the gospel can become a disguise for a "reduction" of it. But there is another and higher sense in which it is but a way of saying that the God of whom the gospel speaks is the God of the whole world, and that the Lord in whom that God so richly dwelt claims "all the kingdoms for his own."

Despite the respect owed to "science" and its achievements, there is a growing anxiety and uncertainty, on the part of many people, about life as a whole. People are ill at ease. What Thoreau called the "quiet sense of desperation" is much more prevalent than the prosperous "front" of modern life might seem to indicate. The very fact of our increased knowledge, thanks to science, and the dangerous power this has given men, may have much to do with the dis-ease. However that may be, this anxiety is the explanation for the appearance of the many cults of "reassurance" or "peace of mind" so popular today. It is, of course, true that these cults cannot, so to speak, "deliver the goods." At best they may be able to give their adherents a temporary sense of well-being and security, at worst they are likely to provide dangerously effective techniques for evading the harsh reality of life as it really is. Like the ostrich in the desert, those who succumb to their appeal may simply hide their heads in the sand while the storms blow. They are trying to escape from the world.

Yet we dare not forget that the Christian gospel does promise peace—not as the world gives it, to be sure, but peace nonetheless. The words of Isaiah are often in my mind: "Thou shalt keep him in perfect peace whose mind is stayed on thee, because he trusteth in thee." This ancient prophet's affirmation was drawn from the depths of his own experience of the anchorage that faith in God had provided for his life. To the Christian it should come with renewed power. For our gospel is that in the person of Jesus Christ, and through a total surrender to him and a life lived in him, God has provided for us a basic security among the changes and chances of this mortal life. So it is that in our "given" world, and to the people who dwell in it here and now, the gospel is not only challenge and demand but also the "peace of God which passeth all understanding."

It will require all our ingenuity to distinguish, both for ourselves and for our people, between the specious "peace of mind" of the cults and the abiding "peace of God" which follows upon acceptance of the proclamation of Christ as Lord. Yet we are compelled to this effort, for we must make clear to our people in this day of confusion, anxiety, and disquietude, that in their Christian faith, as they respond in heart and mind and soul and will to the love of God declared and shown in Christ Jesus, there is a steadying power that will enable them to take life as it comes and to make of it, by God's grace, a thing of beauty, of dignity, and of glory. The parson who talks about these things but who in his own life is a fussy, bothered, anxious, and confused person, will teach quite the opposite of what his lips are saying. This is why it is incumbent upon us, not only for our own salvation but above all for those whose joy, as St. Paul puts it, we are commissioned to help, that we develop in ourselves a deep and rich and serene life of Christian faith and devotion. A preacher of the gospel without *that* is a preacher without the "one thing needful."

This leads directly to another element in the pattern of our times. It is plain that men and women today, again perhaps largely because of the scientific temper, but perhaps also for much deeper reasons, tend to be pragmatic in temper. They judge by results. Many of us are likely to believe that such pragmatism is essentially unchristian and therefore dismiss it out of hand. I cannot think this right. "By their fruits ye shall know them," our Lord said; and it seems to me to be part of the Christian claim for the gospel of Christ that acceptance of our Lord as Master of our lives does produce results. Dean Inge once remarked that "faith is an experiment that ends in an experience"; and we need to remember that while a cheap and easy judging by results is both dangerous and ignoble, what Baron von Hügel described as "long-range pragmatism"—the slow, gradual, but sure ripening of the fruit—may be both a valuable criterion of truth and a convincing demonstration of it.

The real trouble, of course, is that people today want not only results, but quick results. They are imbued with the idea that immediate consequences must follow from the first, or at most the second or third, application. They are likely "to send the bottle back" to the tradesman if such immediate results do not come. Surely our job here is plain. We must make it clear, in our preaching of the gospel, that like everything that is worth having, Christian "fruits" do not come easily. They must be worked for; they must be given time. We need to be careful not to preach the gospel as if it were a quick panacea for all ills. We must say plainly that nobody became a Christian, and nobody remained one, without putting all of himself into it and studying for a long time in the practice of it. We must ask for the *whole* man. *Then* the results will come.

We dare not give the impression that the gospel is a panacea in still another cheap sense. Sometimes preachers suggest, if they do not actually say, that if everybody should become Christian, all the world's problems would be solved. I have often thought that if everybody did become Christian in a serious commitment to our Lord, our problems would at once be enormously increased. We should then be enabled to see heights and depths of human possibility, of human achievement and of human degradation, which the secularist, the humanist, or the semi-Christian, never even dreams about. Christianity, and the gospel it proclaims, does not and cannot claim to solve every human problem and to answer every human question. What it can claim is that in the gospel we have a perspective in which we see these problems and questions in a new and right way, a sense of proportion which helps us get things in their proper place, and a power which enables us to live as human sons of God rather than as sophisticated simians.

It is important to make this clear from the start. We must not pretend to be able to give more than in fact we can deliver; we must not let people think that the gospel can do for them what it can do for no man and for no age. It is the "power of God unto salvation," not the blue-print for an earthly utopia nor a detailed program for worldly achievement, however good. This is not to say that the gospel is not relevant to the political, economic, social, industrial, national, and international situation. It is relevant to them all, but not in any easy way. It provides us with the ultimate standard: human personality made in the image of God, living in community with the brethren. In terms of that standard, all blueprints and all programs are to be judged. And the gospel provides us with the power—the love of God released in Christ Jesus and made effective in our love for our fellowmen—which enables us to go through toil and hardship in the effort to bring more justice to more men at more times and in more places. Surely that is relevance of the highest order.

Many years ago, when I was a student, I walked in Times Square, New York, with a friend. We were commenting on the drab and dull faces of the city dwellers whom we met on the street. And then there came along the street a young lady of such beauty, poise, and charm, that my friend—rather susceptible in such matters—suddenly said, "Look at her. I guess there's something worthwhile after all." In my more mature years I have found that that incident points to a truth of much deeper significance. When I ride in the New

York subway or on a bus, I am inclined to think how drab and dull, how stupid and inane, much of life is; how hopeless most of the people one meets seem to be. And then, with a turn of the mind, I think of the flaming figure of Jesus Christ, who wore our humanity like a royal garment, who turned the curse of life into a Cross bravely borne, who triumphed not so much over strife as in the midst of strife. And when I think of him, I can look again at the people around me and the world in which they and I live; and then I find that I have for these people and for that world a strange love, a deep concern, an inescapable care. If *he* lived in our world, if *he* wore our human nature, then indeed there is hope. The gospel of God in Jesus Christ gives us precisely this hope; and it also gives us renewed faith in the ordinary man and woman of our towns and cities and villages, and a renewal of love which cannot rest until all men have been given the opportunity to live with dignity and beauty even in our meanest streets, and until those very streets have been made fit highways for the brethren of the Son of the living God.

The gospel is directed at sinners: "I came to call not the righteous, but sinners to repentance." The irony of our Lord's word is found of course in the fact that all men, but *especially* those who think themselves righteous, are sinners. The old evangelical saying, that you can preach salvation only to a man who feels himself convicted of sin, is entirely true and should never be forgotten by any preacher of the gospel of Christ. Yet I must make some qualifications.

Thanks to many factors—the present world situation with its dangers, the frustration which industrialized society creates, the diffused influence of critics such as Reinhold Niebuhr, and many other contributing causes—most men and women in the western world today are quite aware of sin in a general and pervasive sense. They would not use the word "sin," of course, but they would admit that they know the sense of failure, the awareness of estrangement, the feeling of inadequacy to meet the demands of life. All this is real enough to our contemporaries. They may seem on the surface very comfortable in Sion; they may seem interested only in keeping up with their neighbors; they may be conservative politically or they may be self-satisfied with their radicalism. But when we get down underneath that surface, there is exactly what some recent American writers, themselves secularist in point of view, have insistently noted: a sense of loneliness, of lostness, of heavy burdens to be carried. I am thinking of Arthur Schlesinger, Jr., Lionel Trilling, Peter Viereck, and Arthur Koestler; but there are many others like them in other lands, who in book after book have painted our generation for us. What the old, and perhaps now unworkable, concept of "original sin" (and how many of us wish that we had a better and more adequately descriptive phrase!) was intended to portray is as real to them as anything can be.

But what is lacking in these analyses and in the people who are being described is a vivid realization of the equally important fact of *actual sins,* of the particular *this* and *that* which each one of us does and for which each one of us is finally responsible. This is the stuff of our daily experience and yet it must be brought home to us. Here the preacher of the gospel today is presented with a task that will exact every ounce of his energy. He must somehow show the ways in which such men and women as he finds in his congregation, or wherever else he proclaims Christ, are *actually* sinners. It does not do much good to talk about our "state of sin" or our "sense of estrangement"; it is much more important to bring into the foreground the actual commissions and omissions of this man and that man. But we shall not get very far with him if we talk about sin and sins in a strictly "religious" sense. For it is not in the "religious areas" that most people, inside the Church or outside it, do really sin. Of course it is true as a theological statement that sin is a "religious" concept, as we so often hear it said today. What that fact ought to mean is that the common stuff of our sinning, in the places where we actually do sin, is always to be seen—once we are aware of our potential and partly realized God-man relationship—as being in the last analysis "against" God because it is contrary to his will for his children. But in the actual business of sinning we sin against society, our husband, wife, children, parents, classmates, neighbors, business partners and business competitors, against our friends and our enemies, against our talents and abilities. It is true that the man who has understood the gospel knows that "against thee only have I sinned, and done this evil in thy sight." Yes. But the places where he sins, and the kind of sins he commits, are not likely to be religious in the *narrower* sense. Our job as preachers of the gospel is to probe deeply, to awaken in our hearers the sense that in the "given" wrongdoings, wrong-thinkings, wrong-sayings of which they are conscious or can be made conscious, they are demonstrating both their involvement in sinfulness and also expressing their deep need for the gospel of Jesus Christ with its message of pardon, grace, and peace.

Yet even so, the gospel is not about sin; it is about redemption. It is not about the old Adam, in whom all die; it is about the new Adam, in whom all shall be made alive. It is my settled belief that we have had nearly enough preaching which *centers attention* on men's sin; what we need these days is preaching about God's grace. We need the *good* news of what God is, what God has done and still does and will do; we do not need the *bad* news of human failure, wickedness, frustration, evil-doing. We need to hear more about what men may be, what in the divine purpose they really are, what by the grace of our Lord Jesus Christ they may become. We need the preaching of faith in Christ, of hope through him, and of love given by him. That is to say, we need the gospel.

In the period between the wars, North America was swept by a somewhat silly popular song which urged us to "accentuate the positive and minimize the negative." In our preaching of Jesus Christ, we need the positive: God in Christ, Christ in us the hope of glory, the glorious liberty of the sons of God. Here is our task as preachers of the gospel. If we preach so that men and women can see the joy of the Christian life, as the result of acceptance in faith of the Lord whom the gospel proclaims, and if at the same time we who are Christ's ministers demonstrate that joy in our own lives, we shall find a surprising response not only from people inside but from people outside the Church. We must, of course, be sure that the joy is not that spurious and specious thing which makes the "professional Christian" an abomination unto the Lord and an annoyance to his neighbors. The joy of which we speak is the free, spontaneous, overflowing of life in charity, such as marked our Lord himself. Nobody could have called him a gloomy man, although he was certainly a serious one. Nobody could have called him "professionally" religious, although he was certainly one whose life was filled with the divine presence and power. He was a happy man; but his happiness was the blessed happiness of one whose life is hid in God.

The good news of the gospel can bring to our "given" world, and to the lonely, lost, heavy-laden people in it, "joy and peace in believing." If our preaching of the gospel does not do that, there is something radically wrong with our preaching, and very likely something radically wrong with us who are the preachers.

4.

PROBLEMS
IN PROCLAIMING
THE GOSPEL
TODAY

Problems in preaching the gospel today flow out of the necessity for relating the Christian story, the gospel, to the "ordinary knowledge" of the common man. These problems are for the most part theological in nature; and although the *gospel* is not the enunciation of theological propositions, the theology implicit in his preaching of it is of the highest significance for the pastor as he considers his task of bringing the "given gospel" to the "given world."

Moreover, these problems are such that the theologian may be able to say something about them which will be relevant to the whole enterprise of Christian thought and communication, as this is focused in the preaching office of the minister. Often it is what one might call "the background material" which is the most important problem for the preacher. His way of proclaiming the "given" gospel will to a considerable degree be determined by his theological pre-suppositions, by his way of approaching the needs that are felt in our time, and by his understanding of the questions which are raised today and must be faced by Christian thinkers. For these play their part in his preaching, quite as much as does his own personal grasp on the Church's essential gospel.

Earlier we had occasion to note the relationship between Jewish faith as portrayed for us in the Old Testament and the Christian event which is the subject matter of the New Testament; and how it was indeed inevitable and right that the primitive Christian community should see their Lord and apprehend his significance for men, against the background of the whole history of the people into whom humanly speaking he was born. It was natural that they should have interpreted him in the light of that history, finding in him the "Yea" spoken by God to all the promises which, as the Jews had believed and as the early Christians also believed, had been made to Israel. Therefore it was also natural that the *kerygma* as we find it in the New Testament should not only be couched in biblical terms but also that these terms require for their proper understanding an awareness of the whole Old Testament witness and record.

But this historically necessary connection and condition has led many in our own day to feel that the gospel of Christ is exhaustively and completely stated when it has been phrased thus in the language of the Bible. Hence they regard the influence of the Hellenistic tradition upon succeeding centuries of Christian thought as both improper and dangerous. Furthermore, they look with the gravest suspicion upon any attempt made today to speak, to teach, and above all to preach in an idiom which is not in the strictest sense biblical. They assume that "biblical preaching," in the sense of preaching the message of the Bible, must mean the use of "biblical language" and that alone. I am convinced that this position is mistaken; and for two reasons.

In the first place, there is an historical objection. It is a sheer fact, undisputed by any who have knowledge of what transpired in early Christian history, that the Christian Church developed its patterns of thought, its theology, through the constant interaction of the biblical witness and the "non-biblical" environment in which the primitive Christian community found itself. One of the major contributions of recent scholarship to our understanding of the development of Christian ideas has been its demonstration that what we call the Catholic faith, as well as Catholic worship, owed an enormous debt to the Graeco-Roman culture in which it had its existence. But a good deal of this has long been known and it should give no cause for alarm. Not only was the most primitive *kerygma* soon seen in the light of the varied patterns of thought found in wider areas of the Mediterranean world, but the inevitable contacts of the Church with the culture of that world brought new intuitions and perceptions about the *kerygma* itself. Subtly but profoundly these modified the initial ways of stating and apprehending the gospel; indeed we may well say that they gave a new depth to the understanding of Christ and his significance, and even a new content to the original gospel itself, insofar as Christ came to be interpreted in the light of the needs of men and women to whom he was being preached.

Surely this ought not to trouble us, unless we are of that peculiar school of Christian thought which assumes that God speaks only in the Hebrew tongue! For those who are convinced that God "has nowhere left himself without witness," it is part of the glory of Christianity that it can include, and by including be modified by the wider range of the divine self-revelation, without losing its own distinctive and special quality. However we approach the question, it remains true as a matter of simple history that Christianity in its development represents what we might describe as the marriage of Jewish realism and of cultural forms which are not Jewish at all. In this marriage, the well-known words, "What God has joined together, let no man"—not even a "biblical theologian" of the twentieth century—"put asunder."

In the second place, it is plain enough that our congregations today, and even more the people outside the Church whom we wish to reach for the gospel of Christ, are quite unable to follow the intricacies of the prophecy-fulfillment pattern of the Old and New Testaments. They must come to see this *after* they have encountered the gospel itself in all its challenge and with all its empowering. Failure to recognize this simple and patent truth about the people of our time, whether they be educated or uneducated, sophisticated or simple, explains to a large degree the admitted failure of what is compendiously called "neo-orthodoxy" to communicate itself significantly to the ordinary man and woman of our day. Professor Elmer Homrighausen, of the Princeton Seminary, himself inclined in the neo-orthodox direction, wrote about this matter in *The Christian Century* (July 18, 1956):

Through my own pastoral experiences I have come to see that neo-orthodoxy—with all its emphasis on realism in theology, on the *kerygma* of the Bible, on the sinfulness of personal and corporate life, on the radical nature of the new life, and so forth—is hesitant and weak in calling persons to a positive faith.

And he went on to intimate, although he did not say outright, that at least one reason for this hesitation and weakness is that the persons to whom such preaching is addressed are in no condition, intellectually or spiritually, to get the point of the message of the neo-orthodox preacher. Nor can this intellectual and spiritual incapacity be put down simply to the sin of the hearers; rather it is the consequence of a genuine and honest difficulty in understanding. There is a cultural "block" here which somehow must be met. It is the task of the preacher of the gospel to find ways in which he can so translate his message that the block will no longer prevent the challenge of the gospel, its real "offense," from getting across to the people to whom he is addressing himself.

One of the difficulties is quite simply that many feel the clergy to be less than completely honest in matters of this kind. Dean Inge once said that the laity have the right to expect two things, and two things only, from the clergy: "that they will preach the gospel and tell the truth." A considerable number of our contemporaries think that in preaching the gospel the clergy are consciously *not* telling the truth. That is, these people feel that the clergy are not willing to face the full impact of the best thought of our time and the changes which that new situation must make in our ways of thinking. They feel that we are not really interested in the truth in this sense; they consider that our only concern is for winning converts or keeping them once they have been won. To what extent that is true of us I do not venture to say, but it ought not to be true at all. We can profit from a consideration of the verdict which Archbishop Frederick Temple passed on Cardinal Newman (with how much justice I am not able to say): "His initial mistake was that he began by searching for the true church rather than for the truth; he inverted the right order." We are to seek the truth and to preach the truth, for the gospel is really nothing other than the proclamation of him who *is* the Truth; and this ought to imply that we are committed to a recognition and welcoming of truth wherever it is found, and to the glad use of it in the imparting of our Christian message.

Nowhere is our problem so clearly shown as in the question to which Rudolf Bultmann has made the most notable, if not the correct, response. I refer to the whole matter of the biblical world-view or cosmology. A three-storeyed universe, with heaven above, hell beneath, and man and his history located in between the two; a disregarding of secondary causes and hence an emphatic declaration that the divine action and will is the one and only cause of all that happens, both good and ill; a gallery of angelic and demonic figures playing their part in the economy of things; and so much else . . . here we have a way of seeing the world and man's existence in it which has little relation, I should say *no* relation, to what the man and woman of our time believes and knows about both. Bultmann puts it strikingly when he says that in a world where we light our houses by electricity, one cannot meaningfully talk of disease as caused by demons. Precisely. One of the tasks which we face today, as men commissioned to preach the Lord Jesus Christ as God's action for man's wholeness, is the disentangling of the essential gospel from this incredible cosmology.

It is simply not true that the gospel of God in Jesus Christ for man's wholeness stands or falls with this biblical picture of the world. But a great many of our contemporaries honestly think that, for good or for ill, it undoubtedly does. And those of them who hear us preach are quite likely to believe that *we* are not ourselves honest when we preach the gospel, because they know perfectly well that in our "secular" moments we do not subscribe to any such scheme of things. Somehow we must make plain in our preaching that this biblical science, so to say, and the cosmology which goes with it, is not integral to the gospel itself. We must take pains to show that acceptance of Jesus Christ as Lord does not carry with it the three-storey universe; that to be a Christian does not imply that one believes that God is the immediate cause of all that happens, however true it may be that he is "first" and "final" cause; and that the findings of modern science as to how God in fact works in the world only illuminate the central truth that in Christ he has worked with a singular intensity and (as we might say) directness to bring to men wholeness of life.

Furthermore, the gospel inevitably has been associated with mythological ways of stating it which, while entirely appropriate to the times when the association was made, are no longer appropriate today. By my use of the word "mythological" here, I mean nothing derogatory. The language of mythology, or, as I myself prefer to say, metaphor, is the language which religion speaks; it can do no other, for religious faith is neither scientific formulae nor philosophical concepts, but a dramatic, poetic, symbolical way of speaking of the deepest realities and our apprehension of them. We have already argued this point. But, on the other hand, some ways of mythological speaking have had their day and are gone forever. Or, if they are to be retained, their character as metaphorical must be stated clearly, lest they be understood in a literal and prosaic sense and, in consequence, become stumbling blocks to faith and barriers to the acceptance of Christ as Lord.

Bultmann himself has proposed what has been translated as "de-mythologizing" the gospel. The word is highly misleading, for what Bultmann actually wishes to do is not to *remove* the mythology but so to enter into its meaning that it can be restated in terms which he thinks to be significant today. It is his opinion that we can best state the evangelical message and the evangelical demand in the idiom of contemporary existentialism, more particularly by use of the analysis of the human situation made in the writings of the German existentialist philosopher Martin Heidegger. We certainly cannot be without sympathy for some aspects of Bultmann's proposal. But the way to accomplish what he rightly sees to be necessary is by a process which might be described as "in-mythologizing." By this "in-mythologizing," there is the possibility of penetration into the reality which the ancient cosmology and the mythology used by the biblical writers was attempting to state in language appropriate to their time. It is something like this that Bultmann is really seeking after; but his presentation of the project is so entangled with Heideggerian existentialism that the result is not always very clear, even to the instructed reader.

Let us consider first the cosmology of the Bible. What we ought to be able to discover in this world picture, once the incredible science is gone, is a conception of the universe in which, under what are for us weird and frequently utterly impossible images, the whole creation is seen as dependent upon a loving and active God who is its ultimate meaning and its ground of being. Or again, we are enabled to see that the contrasted angelic and demonic hosts suggest the recognition of the fact that man is surrounded and indwelt by "forces" for good and by "forces" for evil; there are "graces" which raise man up, as well as "drives" which push him down, and any realistic man lives constantly in a situation where he must decide for or against the good which is finally from God, which indeed finally *is* God.

Something of the same process follows in respect to the "mythology." We read of the "comings down" and the "goings up" which are more immediately associated with the gospel: "he came down from heaven," "he rose again from the dead," "he ascended into heaven," and the like. Here the whole set of images is of a highly mythological sort, doubtless related to "redeemer myths" and other primitive, or sometimes more sophisticated, schemes of thought. These images seem almost inextricably linked with the *kerygma* as it was first proclaimed and understood. But such ideas and pictures no longer have meaning. We cannot hope to make our people see what the gospel of Christ says to them today, unless we engage for them in the task of translating this out of the imagery in which it was first stated. It is perfectly possible for us, and hence for those who hear our preaching, to get so bogged down in the traditional biblical picture, taken in its most literal form, that the whole point of the gospel itself is lost.

In this situation it is helpful to discriminate between the kinds of language which are used in Christian discourse.* In the first place, while the language of religion is meta-

* For a fuller treatment of this theme, see Pittenger, *The Word Incarnate* (New York: Harper & Bros., 1959), pp. 33-44.

phorical, this blanket statement needs to be broken down so that we see that certain distinctive forms of speech are appropriate to certain distinctive kinds of biblical reference. The story of creation and the story of the fall, for example, like the account of the last things in the Book of Revelation, may properly be called *myths,* since they are concerned with absolute beginnings and endings or with universally predicable truths, about which no precise conceptual statements can be made and which are best expressed in pictorial language. But the Christian gospel is in a very different category; it has to do with historical event and is in the form of an *epic* or a *saga* or a *story.* It should not be described as a "myth," for despite a proper use of the word which might be permissible, there is a serious danger of a misunderstanding of it since generally its meaning is taken to be a "fairy-tale"—a symbolic account of what may be most dreadfully "un-fact." The story, the epic, the saga, which tells about, and interprets the significance of, the life of Christ and his work for men, is of course told in a metaphorical idiom and might be described as mythological so far as its *manner of telling* is concerned. But genuine facts which actually did occur, real historicity, a Jesus who walked the ways of this earth and by his impact on men evoked from them the faith to which Christians subscribe, are basic to it all, and without such factuality it would have a meaning entirely different from that significance which Christians claim for it. And last, there are *legendary tales,* associated with the Christian story but not integral to its historical reality. These tales, which the form-critics would call "wonder" or "miracle" pericopes, have gathered around the saga and are closely related to its factuality. They are *not* unimportant, as some have said, for they are part of the evidence we possess as to the impression which Jesus made upon men. Without them we should have far less than that full impression, even though their precise historical verisimilitude may be open to grave question.

We preachers of the gospel must first see for ourselves, and then we must help our people to see, that it is wrong to take language that is symbolically apt and use it as if it were language that is philosophically and scientifically precise. To take an illustration from another area, we speak for example of man's being, in Luther's phrase, "twisted in on himself" (*incurvatus in se*). This is certainly correct enough if we do not take it literally. And we go on to say that only as this proud self-concern, this inversion of life upon the false self as its center, is "broken into" by the divine love, can man be saved. But we ought not to assume that this perfectly sound way of phrasing things, for the purpose of describing the experience of "salvation," is scientifically accurate, or is literally the truth. Or again, when we speak in the creed of the Eternal Word of God as "coming down from heaven," we surely do not think—or at least we ought not to think—that this is a precise statement of movement from an "up" to a "down"; we all know well enough that it is, on the contrary, a most inaccurate statement from that point of view. It is a metaphorical statement, true in its own poetical fashion; it is a most valuable way of saying in symbolical language, that he who is supreme in the order of being was for our sakes willing to be united to and self-expressed in the life of the Brother-Man who is therefore our Lord and Saviour, Emmanuel, God-with-us.

This brings vividly before us still another aspect of our

problem. One of our greatest difficulties in preaching today comes from the widespread notion that in Jesus Christ, and indeed in all situations where God is believed to be especially "at work," we have what is often described as an "intrusion" from outside the world into the order of events with which we are commonly familiar. A number of distinguished Christian theologians and many popular apologists continually talk in this fashion. Mr. C. S. Lewis may be cited, for one of the apologists; and the theologians are legion. But is this kind of metaphor a very useful one today? Does it not lead to much misunderstanding as to what is *really* meant? One is tempted to ask, when such words as "intrusion" and the ideas that seem inevitably associated with such words are used, "From *where,* then, does God intrude?" Is not this whole mode of thought simply part of the evil legacy from deism, in which God was conceived as being absent from his world, and in which therefore he must be thought to "intrude" into his world, to "intervene" in it, whenever he would act in any distinctive and particular way? Surely, however, the basic affirmation of Christian theism, founded (once we have got behind the images in which often it was phrased) on the biblical witness to the faithfulness and consistency of God and to his unfailing maintenance of the creation in being, is that all things at all times and in all places are present to God, that he is always at work in them, that he constantly energizes through them, that he never ceases to move in the creation towards the accomplishment of his holy will and the revelation of his holy purpose. Thus it is plain that he does not need to "come into the world" from outside it; he is already here. If he were not, there would be no world at all. He "upholds all things by the word of his power," and ceaselessly operates in them and through them. What he does do, in this process, is to act with greater or less intensity at this or that place. He operates with subtle and sometimes extraordinary vigor *here* rather than *there,* thus bringing to pass his "work, his strange work" both in the order of nature and of history, and thus bringing to pass also his loving care and saving action signally declared in Jesus Christ. Once again, we should be on our guard lest language, which may now and again be liturgically apt and poetically appropriate, be taken in our preaching as if it were literal and precise. And above all, we should be on our guard against preaching a gospel in which the God who is proclaimed as active in Christ is other than the God who is the Lord of all creation.

In conclusion, the point should be reiterated that to say that the gospel of Christ is to be stated in language which is avowedly metaphorical does not in any sense whatever imply that the gospel is not true. Nor does it mean that, in preaching the gospel in conscious recognition of the metaphorical nature of the language we use, we are speaking in what might be styled a "Pickwickian" manner. On the contrary it is only by this honest recognition that we can make the truth of the gospel come alive to our contemporaries. They are not quite so stupid as some would think; they know perfectly well the distinction between literal speech which has an almost one-to-one correspondence with the facts, and metaphorical speech in which the truth is so vast and mysterious that no set of words can do other than give intimations, suggestions, and indications of the reality that is being spoken. Religious language is poetry, if you will; but it is poetry because "the dimension of depth" in religion (to borrow Dr.

Tillich's phrase) can be spoken only by poetry. Furthermore, when in faith we are describing historical fact in all its enormous wealth of meaning—as we are doing when we preach Christ as bringing God's presence and grace to men in singular and decisive fashion—we are bound to put this in language whose metaphorical quality is inevitable. But this should suggest to us that the reality to which we point is such that there is but one way to apprehend it: not by cold logic, philosophical concept, literal precision, rational explanation, but by what we have always known was required —the commitment of the whole person to this reality, the heart's surrender to Christ as God's self-expression in human life for the recovery of man's wholeness and for his abiding joy.

Closely related to the foregoing problem is the question of "miracle." Here we need to speak very carefully, because there is one sense in which "miracle," once we have rightly understood what that term means in its deepest signification, is the heart of religion. But that is not the sense in which the common man, and a large group of the clergy too, I fear, do in fact understand it. Unhappily, they tend to think of miracle as signifying an arbitrary intrusion into, a suspension of, or an interference or interruption in (the last two words are Mr. C. S. Lewis's), the regular course of events in the world of nature. Surely there can be no doubt at least that the average layman thinks that this is what is intended; and he assumes that when the clergy speak of miracle, this is precisely what they mean.

Such is not, however, the conception of miracle which was taught by the great theologians of the Church. The truth is that this common notion of miracle is but another bad legacy from the age of deism, a subtle form of that deism persisting in the minds of ordinary people and also (alas!) in the minds of some sophisticated modern theologians who like to consider themselves highly "orthodox." But we can say at least this: the essential meaning of the concept of the miraculous as this has been used in traditional theology, is grounded in the keen awareness men have of the unexpected and unprecedented experiences and happenings, the novel and hence the unusually stimulating events or circumstances of life, through which men in every age have been aroused to faith in God and have been given a deepening conviction of his love and care. In this sense a miracle speaks of what Gerard Manley Hopkins so beautifully called "the dearest freshness deep down things." Life is not on a dead and uniformitarian level; it contains moments of less and of greater intensity. If this meaning is preserved, it will not be necessary for us to haggle over the historical probability and the likely evidence for the stories of miraculous events in the Bible, even for the miracle stories in the New Testament and in association with the life of our Lord himself. We shall have the root of the matter in us; we shall have come to recognize that in the history leading up to our Lord, and with the coming of Jesus himself, there were released into the world, and that in what we may rightly call an unprecedented fashion, energies for good which have changed the lives of men and through them the face of nature too, and that these same energies are still available whenever men turn, in faith and with utter self-surrender, to the Lord of all life.

For myself, I am frank to say, I could wish that the *word* "miracle," as a theological term, were abandoned. It has had its day. In our contemporary situation, it is so encumbered with the legacy from deism, of which I have spoken, that its use is calculated to bring out all the wrong ideas of its meaning and to put enormous obstacles in the way of acceptance of the gospel. Nor is it without significance that the word as such does not occur in the gospels save in one or two places. In the gospels we have *semeion* or sign, and *dunamis* or power, and only once or twice *terata* or wonders. Dr. William Porcher DuBose seems to suggest in his fine autobiography *Turning Points of My Life,* and James Matthew Thompson explicitly said in his *Through Fact to Faith*— both of these books are nearly a half-century old—that the soundly biblical conception of *providence* serves to safeguard and to state all that the term "miracle" was once used to affirm. It is too bad that this has not been more generally accepted. For "providence" is a word which tells us of the conviction that God exercises a never-failing and personal control over, even as he unfailingly works within, the events and circumstances of life, molding them and molding us in such a way that his grace and power are manifested in human history and in personal experience. Furthermore we are accustomed to recognize that God's providential care and action are not all on one level; there are the regularities and there are the "high points," so to say, the moments of less and the moments of greater intensity. And for the Christian faith, the claim to be made is that the moment of greatest intensity is the emergence in the sphere of history and of human life of the person of Jesus Christ, with all that he was and all that he continues to be, all that he did and all that he continues to do, all that he meant and all that he continues to mean for those who respond to him in heart's surrender. Here, then, is special providence, par excellence; and it is special not by its being removed from all relationship to God's more general providence in ordering, controlling, and caring for nature and history and the lives of men, but by the heightening and focussing in that one moment in history or in human life of what God everywhere and always is "up to."

As in a reading glass the rays of the sun may be focussed and thus intensified, without in any way denying or darkening those rays as they shine down upon, say, the whole garden, so in Christ God's loving concern in focussed and thus intensified, not by denying but by concentrating his other and wider operation. The result of that focussing in Christ is *fire,* the fire of love of God and of men made in grateful response to Christ and to what he does for those who accept him. Our task and our privilege as those commissioned to preach the gospel is to make exactly this clear and compelling to our hearers. We can do this most effectively if we see to it that the dubiously historical "wonders" with which it has been associated are no longer made central to its significance, even while we still recognize and value the testimony that all these give to the impact which God has made through Christ upon the lives of those who knew and know him.

In the second place, the point of view which would insist upon an absolute distinction between Jesus Christ and all other instances of divine revelation is not confined to the so-called "neo-orthodox." While it is of course true that those who belong to this school are perhaps most vocal in their assertion that in our Lord alone may God be seen at work, and while it is they who denounce the concept of "general" revelation as a vain fancy of sub-Christian speculation, a considerable number of other Christian thinkers take what in effect is the same position when they make central to their teaching a kind of uniqueness in the coming and the person of Christ which effectively removes him from the context of the total self-expressive operation of the Eternal Word. And in the preaching of the gospel this same notion frequently shows itself, when the minister who proclaims in Christ the action of God for man's wholeness puts our Lord in a total isolation from other men in whom something of the divine activity is at work. For one of the most frequent emphases in contemporary theology, and consequently in a good deal of contemporary preaching, is that there is (what is styled) an absolute "difference in kind" between the self-expression of God in and through any and every man, and that which was accomplished in Jesus Christ our Lord. Such a position is theologically unsound and homiletically disastrous. In saying this I am in no sense succumbing to the so-called "unitarian" levelling-down of all God's revelation to one uniform method and way. There is nothing whatever to be said for that view, which indeed should be described not as "unitarian" but as "uniformitarian." Any honest survey of the situation makes clear that there are very considerable differences in the movement of God in and through nature, history, and human life. God is more intensively at work, more actively present, in this or that place than in these or those other places.

The point here, however, is that the view that our Lord is *absolutely* different in kind from any and every other work and presence of God is impossible to maintain, and that for several reasons. It is impossible because, for one thing, such an absolute difference in kind as is often proposed would carry with it the corollary that there is no way in which we are able to recognize what God was "up to" in Christ when we meet him there. In fact, there would be no way in which we could recognize God as being there at all. That which is *absolutely different,* as Aristotle implied long ago, is *unknowable.* There must be *some* kind of continuity in experience if genuine knowledge is to be possible. Furthermore, this kind of preaching and teaching tends to make the Incarnation of God in Christ an unrelated wonder or prodigy which, because it has no relation to the totality of the divine action, cannot reveal the eternal purposes of God; all too often, such a position is associated with a sophisticated modern kind of Marcionism, that leads to a contempt for the Old Testament in its own integrity and for the revelation of God found there quite apart from its fulfillment in Christ. If our Lord has no genuine and close relationship with those whom he was willing to call his brethren, then it would seem that that which was "determined, dared, and done" in him, to use Christopher Smart's stupendous verbs, is but done *to* us and hence is unshared and unshareable by those who are in common Christian experience given the power to live "in him."

Indeed, we can best understand the difference between Jesus Christ and his human brethren in whom God (by definition of theistic faith itself) is in some manner present and energizing, as the difference between that One in whom God lived, acted, and expressed himself in the fullest adequacy which we can conceive possible in human life and experience (while it remains genuine human life and experience), and those in whom that same God is indeed at work, as the necessary ground of their life and the invisible secret of their action, but in whom his energizing is, as we might say, of lower intensity and with less adequacy. The reason for this difference is not only that in these others God's energizing is blocked by human willfulness and sin. *More important* and *more basic* than that, it is because God's own purpose of self-expression does not there expect and provide for such adequacy as was achieved by him once for all in human regard, when by his prevenient preparation, his concomitant grace, and his effectual action he was "made flesh" in the person of Jesus Christ. Here, as Karl Barth has rightly maintained, is the signal instance of divine "election." Jesus Christ is the "Elect One," not by some effort of human nature alone, for that would not be real election, but by God's eternal purpose which "from the beginning of the world"— and long before it, too, if we may so speak—has determined that "in the fulness of the times" there shall be just such an actualization of the potential God-Man relationship as Christian faith discerns in Christ our Lord. Such a position I believe to be within the limits of Christian orthodoxy, and especially of some of the great Patristic teaching—although certainly not within the limits of much modern neo-orthodoxy, whether Catholic or Protestant. But that is another case where a view that is fashionable in many circles today, and likes to call itself alone properly "orthodox," is sometimes surprisingly close to an ancient heresy.

Some may think that all this is irrelevant to the preaching of the gospel. I cannot agree. It is precisely after we have made an effort to face such problems as these that we can bring the *kerygma* in all its glory to the people with whom we have to do. There is no salvation in telling men that Jesus is an "intruder" from another world, who has not really shared our condition because, as an alien, he is not in fact one of us. But there is great salvation in proclaiming that

God in Christ has accomplished the purpose for which man was made, and through which his weakness and failure, his sin and shame, are overcome. That purpose is that God may be known and loved, worshipped and served, in the Man Christ Jesus, in whom he is made so vividly and poignantly plain to us, and that as a result he may fill our lives with his grace and conform us to his image. In Christ we have the Diamond, "immortal Diamond" (in Gerard Manley Hopkins' noble phrase), while in us we have but the charcoal; yet the two—Diamond and charcoal—are of the same stuff, for both are carbon; and it is by the action of that Diamond upon this charcoal, that the carbon—the God-man relationship which in its full adequacy is found in Jesus Christ—may be seen for what it is, and that we who are the charcoal may be taken into the life of him the Diamond, as men who are "in Christ" for now and for eternity. The analogy, of course, is imprecise and even inaccurate, for diamond does not work upon charcoal in this fashion; yet the *point* of the analogy is clear enough and is the right point to make.

Indeed, we may do enormous harm and often deter those who would come to an acceptance of our Lord, when we insist that they must *begin* their acceptance with complete assent to the fully developed Christian affirmation that he is truly divine as well as truly human. With the disciples, surely, it was otherwise; it was through the wounds of his humanity, as a French Roman Catholic writer once remarked, that the disciples came to the intimacy of his divinity. It is likely that this will also be the way with a considerable number of our contemporaries. They may, for the moment, discount the claim that in him God is truly present for their wholeness; but at least they are willing to say that they find in him the highest and best manhood that any of us can know and that they will give him their hearts and seek to follow in the "blessed steps of his most holy life." We who proclaim Christ ought to have enough faith that our Lord *is* what we *claim* him to be, to permit such men and women to have, if not full then some limited, participation in Christian life in the community of faith; for we are confident, or we should be confident if we really believe what we say about Jesus, that such fellowship with him in the company of his people will lead them more and more deeply into the true significance of his person. We can have confidence that they will be brought sooner or later to say, "My Lord and my God." If we do not believe that this is true, then we had better admit that Christianity is false from the start; and we had better stop preaching it altogether.

It is for these reasons, among others, that more emphasis is needed today on the wonder and glory of Jesus' humanity. Let us admit, as we must, that our knowledge of that humanity comes to us "from faith to faith." Let us admit too that it is a knowledge which is not precise in detail, but is very much more like a painted portrait than a photographic snapshot. Still the fact remains that we do know quite enough about the historic life of Jesus to catch something of his filial obedience to God, his loving concern for men, his unceasing following of the will of his Father, and his equally unceasing desire to bring the Father's shepherding care home to his children. A good deal of the time we may find it useful to begin there; and our preaching of the gospel, once it does begin there, can then move on with the profound logic of experience to the bold affirmation that in *this* Man, in all his human conditioning, God is discovering himself to us as at no other time and in no other place.

We have already noted the necessity for a "point-of-contact" between the gospel and the patterns of thought of contemporary people. Some German theologians would deny that there can be such a "point-of-contact." The gospel, they say, comes as condemnation of sin; and since, in the definition of these theologians, men are utterly alienated from God and entirely estranged from God's purpose, nothing in ordinary experience can be of use in relating the gospel to their situation. This position would seem to be an almost blasphemous denial both of the goodness of God and of his common sense. The creation is always God's creation; and we do not honor him if we assume that he has let it get so completely out of hand that nothing of him is still to be found in it. Historical Christianity, as a matter of fact, has taken a quite different line. It has said that the whole experience of man in its every phase—from the genius of the artist and scientist and poet and thinker, to the commonplace life of the family and the daily round of the office and shop and school, not to speak of nature and its beauty, its regularity, its predictability, its reliability—is all in its way and in its degree a means for the divine self-revelation. It has gloried in the divine activity in what we may call the "secular world."

That is why we who are preachers of the gospel of Christ may seek for the homeliest and simplest, as well as for the most exalted and sublime, analogies for "gospel truth" in the life and work of our people. That also is why the experiences of human life, with all its perversions and distortions, may yet be used as a proper illustration—and it was so used by our Lord himself—for the divine charity in its outreach to men. And that is why human relationships may be taken, as our Lord took them, as analogous to man in his relationship with the ultimate source of his being. We need to remember how our Lord constantly employed in his teaching such homely, and such sublime, analogies: "if ye then . . . how much more." It is the "how much more" that makes the difference, of course; the *a fortiori* is essential to the parable. But yet, the fact remains that in man's "common" experience, in those very human and historical—and sinful—limitations we know so well, we have the right to find in parabolic fashion creaturely representations of that which God is, and that which God has done, and that which God purposes to bring to pass in and for and through and with and to this his world and the men and women whom he has placed in it.

Thus we can move away from that kind of preaching in which our whole time is devoted to telling men what "rotters" they are, and come to the point where we can assure them of the wonder and glory of God's purpose for them. The gospel is indeed concerned to make us all see how terribly estranged we are from the God who is yet present with us. But it is *chiefly* concerned to tell men what they may become in Christ, what indeed they already are in the divine intention: sons of God, made in his image, fallen into sin by their willfulness, and now by the grace of our Lord Jesus Christ able to be conformed to his likeness, the evil and the sin which they know so well being done away through God's forgiving love shed abroad through him.

Finally, we have the problem of the "finality" of Christianity. We are not called upon to claim that *our* Christianity, in its present institutional form and in its present empirical dress, or in any other historical shaping which may be given it, is final and absolute. The only real finality is Jesus Christ himself, the Lord whom the gospel proclaims, and those corollaries of the gospel which are so immediately associated with him that without them he would not be himself. And the finality of Jesus Christ, in whom true God is active for the wholeness of men, consists in his endless fertility; as a modern saint has put it, "He is adequate," and his adequacy is not for us alone but for all men everywhere and at every time. If Jesus is what the gospel proclaims him to be—that One in whom the love and light and life of God possessed completely a genuine human life, possessed it so fully that we may say of him, as Mr. Basil Willey has well phrased it, that "the life of God is seen in him in human life"—then we can preach Jesus Christ as decisive, as definitive, as the norm for the God-man relationship and the clue to whatever else God may be purposing and accomplishing in this vast and mysterious creation.

That, I suppose, is the basic meaning, religiously speaking, of the creedal word *homo-ousion,* "of one substance with the Father." As a matter of theology, the word asserts that "whatever is divine" in Jesus, his deity, is as truly and fully divine as very God himself; but as a matter of religious conviction and experience, it is the assertion that very God, in all his mystery and in all his glory, is of "one substance with," is the same reality as, that which in Jesus Christ we have been given to see and know and touch and feel. So we dare to say, with the Johannine writer, that "God is light, and in him is no darkness at all."

Some wise words of the former Regius Professor of Divinity in the University of Cambridge are helpful to us in thinking of all these matters. Writing on "Bible and Dogma," Dr. John Burnaby has said:

It should be the work of Christian teachers in every generation, first, to understand the Scriptures, to distinguish what gives unity to the message of the Bible from what is peculiar to this or that writer, what is central from what is peripheral, what is essential from what is accidental; and then, on the basis of such understanding, to develop a doctrine of the act of God in Christ which will be intelligible, or at least not meaningless, to the contemporary mind.

If that is the "work of Christian teachers," how much more does it indicate to us the nature of the task which is set for Christian preachers!

Our task, as those who would be faithful preachers of the Word of God, is to bring to our people the Lord Jesus Christ, so that they may share in his "grace and truth." This task we perform in the setting of the Church, whose gospel we proclaim. But we preach to people in *this* day and age, and we must be aware of the problems which face us as we seek loyally to mediate the everlasting gospel to them in their condition. Christ cannot fail, even if we can and do. Our only hope is in his using us, in all our weakness, for the fulfillment of his great purpose, that men may have "life in him."

5.

THE
GOSPEL
EXPRESSED
IN WORSHIP

Our concern thus far has been the centrality and importance of the office of preaching the gospel in the ministry of the Christian Church. We have insisted that the Word of God incarnate in Christ and proclaimed in "the preaching" is constitutive of the Church; and thus we have been in full agreement with generally accepted Reformed doctrine. The Word of God in Christ, primarily declared in the Church's *kerygma,* is what in fact establishes the Church. But at the same time we have insisted, again with the great Reformers of the sixteenth century, as well as with the whole of historical Christianity in its Catholic expression, that there is another side to the picture. We have maintained that the Church's celebration of the sacraments, and especially of the Lord's Supper, in obedience to the command which the New Testament represents our Lord as himself giving, is also fully and genuinely a proclamation of the gospel of Christ. As the Church makes the *anamnesis* or "remembrance" of Christ in its eucharistic action, our Lord Jesus Christ becomes present to it as the very One whom the preaching announces; and thus the Holy Communion, with due regard to its many aspects, is nothing other than the public work—the *liturgy,* as the Greek has it—which establishes the presence of the Lord of the gospel, who here makes himself available to his people and thus constitutes them as his Body, his Church, united with him through Baptism and participant in his life through the reception of the mystery of his "spiritual body and blood."

It is appropriate, therefore, that we should devote at least one chapter to the meaning and place of the Eucharist, and with special emphasis upon the ways in which that celebration enacts what the gospel affirms. Otherwise there would be a suggestion of imbalance, of disproportion, even of distortion of the Christian Church's action combining the "preaching of the Word" and the "administration of the Sacraments." We need always to remember that ministers in Christ's Church are by common consent set apart precisely for the double task of declaring the "pure Word of God" and celebrating the Lord's Supper according to Christ's command and ordinance.

In the Athanasian Creed, that ancient canticle of Christian faith still found in the service books of many Christian communions, there is a fine statement which gives the proper setting for any discussion of Christian worship and, a fortiori, for a discussion of the central act of Christian worship, the sacrament of the Lord's Supper, the Eucharist, the Holy Communion, the Divine Mysteries, the Liturgy, the Mass—call it what you will. The statement runs: "Now the Catholic faith is this: that we worship one God in Trinity, and Trinity in Unity."

At first sight that may seem to be a startling assertion. The faith *is* the worship? But when we come to think about it, surely we come to see that this must be the case. It is not simply that *lex orandi* and *lex credendi,* the Christian rule of praying and the Christian rule of believing, go hand in hand; there is here a more profound truth than that. The deeper truth is that the Christian gospel and the faith which it evokes do, as a matter of fact, bring us to the place where our only response is worship; and a faith which does not involve and express itself in the worship of God through Christ is a faith which is radically imperfect—so imperfect, indeed, that one may doubt that it is true Christian faith at all. On the other hand, the worship which Christians offer to God known in Christ is entirely dependent on the reality which the gospel proclaims and to which faith responds. It is *that* God, known in *that* way, who evokes the response of worship. In this sense, then, the *faith* is *worship*; the two are so much one that it is as impossible for us to believe in God without worshipping him, as it is to worship him without commitment in faith to him. Worship is an integral element in the whole Christian complex; it is central to the life of the Christian believer.

Furthermore, the Christian is one who does not worship God in solitude or isolation, although of course he may and must on occasion adore him without the actual *physical* presence of fellow believers. The Christian is one whose worship is always in company with the whole body of "faithful people," for to be a Christian means to be a member of

Christ, a participant in the community of faith, and thus in profound and never-failing association with his fellow members. It is for this reason that the typical form of Christian worship is social in nature. Unlike adherents to some of the other religions which have commanded the allegiance of men, Christian believers are gathered together as a fellowship, meeting at specific times and in specific places to engage in the action of divine worship.

So far, probably all Christians would agree. But there is a distinctive type of worship which has been continuous within the Christian tradition and which has won the approval of the vast majority of those who are part of that tradition. This is *liturgical* worship. It is worship by and through a *liturgy*. It is with this type of worship that we are concerned in this chapter—and appropriately so, because it is the type of worship which provides the best setting for the preaching of the gospel or Word of God, while at the same time it is the type of worship which best delivers the body of believers from complete dependence upon the minister to whom is committed by the Church both the preaching of the gospel and the conduct of the divine service itself.

The word "liturgy" is derived from the Greek *leitourgeia,* which means "a public work." In ancient Greece, a liturgy was any service rendered or offering made for the good of the community; it did not originally have a specifically religious connotation. But it was natural that the word should be used to describe religious exercises, since these too were usually a "public work," paid for by some public-minded citizen. They were thus "liturgical" in nature, intended for the whole community; and as, say, in the production of a drama with religious overtones, they were both religious in nature and social in character. So it was that the worship of the Christian Church in its early days, a worship of God which was not individual but for the community, and thus marked by a social quality, could be described as a liturgy. The worship of the Church which was offered by the community and intended for all its members was liturgical worship.

The possibility of a common participation in the divine service through the development of set-forms which could be followed by all those who were present, gave liturgical worship a definite structure. It was public; it was communal; it was something in which all the members could share, both by word spoken and by action performed. In describing such worship as "public," we do not mean, of course, that it was opened to all and sundry, but rather that it was public *for the Church* and for all members of the Church who by their baptism had been initiated into the community and thus had been given the status which made it possible for them to participate in what went on when the community engaged in its regular worship of God in Christ.

In the widest sense, then, we may say that liturgical worship is any worship in which, through the use of established and accepted forms, the Christian community as a whole engages in the adoration of God. But there is a narrower sense in which the word "liturgy" has commonly been employed. In the Eastern Orthodox communions and among some other Christian groups, the word "liturgy" is used par excellence to describe the celebration of the Holy Communion. This for them is *the* Liturgy; and whatever other services of worship are held are arranged round it as a center, since they prepare for or are consequent upon the *anamnesis* or "continual remembrance" of Christ in the eucharistic rite. It is appropriate that the name should be given this special eucharistic significance, since of all the occasions when Christians gather together to worship God none is so central, none so charged with high meaning, as the repetition of the actions which Jesus Christ himself performed "on the night in which he was betrayed." Here, as we shall be seeing, the Christian community comes together to be made into the unity which is described in the phrase, "the Body of Christ." Here there is common participation in the liturgical re-enactment of the Last Supper. Here there is entrance into the "benefits"—the results made available for the lives of men —which Christ's life, death, and resurrection effected and which gave rise to the specifically Christian claim that he is God's Son, that One in whom True God dwells supremely in a true man, for the wholeness of all men.

One chief characteristic of liturgical worship, understood both in the wider and the narrower sense, is that it is ordered according to plan and therefore provides for a regular and undeviating repetition of word and action such as shall enable those present to participate in it as fully as possible. There is a very prevalent misunderstanding, especially on the part of those not familiar with this mode of divine service, which assumes that there is something highly ornate about liturgical worship. On the contrary, such worship is really marked by a great simplicity—the simplicity which comes from need for common participation. It is indeed true that often enough the ceremonial action and the prescribed words of the service have a notable richness; but this richness is incidental to the main emphasis, which is consistency, orderliness, regular repetition of word and action, in order to make the service familiar to the people and not a matter of constant surprise, constant change, constant novelty.

In consequence of this regular ordering a liturgical service is marked by a certain dignity and beauty. Dignity and beauty are a natural corollary of form, just as vulgarity and ugliness are often a natural consequence of formlessness. Pattern and plan tend to such dignity and beauty which, in a phrase used in a very different connection by the British art critic Clive Bell, are the result of "significant form." It is always a danger that this dignity and beauty and the form upon which they rest, may be without the warmth of personal participation by the members of the worshipping congregation; then there is "formality" in the bad sense, and there may be a "coldness" which almost amounts to indifference. But I believe that this is very infrequently found. Those who are not accustomed to participation in liturgcial worship are sometimes not able to understand the way in which, for a congregation which is deeply familiar with the prescribed procedures, the repeated words and actions come to have enormous evocative significance. For those who know them, the same canticles, the same versicles and responses, the same collects and lections, used over and over again, have a power to speak to depths of the personality which are not always reached by that which is entirely new and sometimes reeks of the spirit of contemporaneity.

And again, liturgical worship has about it what we may call, following Rudolf Otto, a "numinous" quality. Through the repeated forms as well as through long usage, such worship establishes an atmosphere which speaks of the things of God, and which awakens the sense of the "holy," the "Other." One reason for this is, of course, that the actual liturgies—the forms which are employed in the conduct of such worship—are not new creations; in almost every instance they are adaptations of ancient and hallowed usages, freighted with the devotion of the ages, and they manage to convey suggestions which are much deeper than mere verbalization. Indeed one might say that liturgical worship by and large speaks not so much to the conscious attention of its participants as to those profound and almost unconsciously experienced areas of human life where men live in terms of feeling-tone, of unutterable emotion, and of profound subconscious relationships, with an almost intuitive awareness of the "more" which is deep down in the structure of reality. It is not true that liturgical worship entirely fails to speak to the strictly conscious levels of human experience; it does indeed speak to these, but it has richer connotations and implications; and it is these which do most of the "work" in liturgical as distinguished from didactic or other types of Christian worship.

Still another important aspect of liturgical worship is the way in which it manifests a certain rounded or balanced covering of the whole content of the Christian faith. By such devices as the Church Year, with its rich variety of feasts and fasts, with its commemoration of the events in the life of Christ, and with its concentration at this or that moment on this or that particular Christian affirmation, as well as by the repetition of this variety from year to year, the worshipper is delivered from a certain "choosiness" on the part of the minister, and also from undue centering of attention on some single aspect of the whole Christian affirmation. He gets "into the swing"; and as he goes round and round, over and over again, he is enabled to enter into the fullness of the historic faith, in all its facets and with all the demands that each of its facets makes upon him. Furthermore, the fact that the worshipper himself is involved in all this, that he has his own "liturgy" or expected part to play within the great liturgy of the Church as a whole—his own work to do as a member of the company—and that he is well acquainted with what is going to happen next in the course of the service, delivers him from the vagaries of the minister, who in such worship is not able to obtrude his personality and his personal predilections in any offensive sense.

Liturgical worship does not necessarily require a special type of building or the use of special kinds of ornaments. Yet it is unquestionably true that it naturally lends itself to such. A church building in which the worship is liturgical in nature is almost bound to be a building in which the center of interest, the focus, is not the pulpit but the Holy Table. It is almost bound to be a building in which the arrangements for seating are conducive to full congregational participation. It is almost bound to lead to common actions in which those present will kneel, stand, bow, and the like, thus enabling them to express for themselves the spirit of the whole liturgical action. The congregation has *something to do,* which more fully incorporates them into the whole meaning of what is going on.

Liturgical worship, both because it has been planned and built upon the riches of the Christian heritage and because it almost inevitably leads to an altar-centered church building, is theocentric in emphasis. The minister who conducts the service, if he knows his business, does not attempt to obtrude his personal idiosyncrasies into the worship of God, although it is of course inevitable that he shall be himself—a man, and necessarily this or that man, whose manner of taking the service will in some sense reflect his understanding of what he is doing. The congregation is not there primarily to be edified or instructed, although that certainly will be one of the results of the service. Certainly it is right and essential that a sermon proclaiming the gospel of Christ be one part of the total action. And the fact that the pulpit is set up and the gospel is proclaimed give the Word of God its necessary place in the whole. Yet the direction of worship is towards God; and everything that is done, even the preaching of the Word which is included in the service, will ultimately tend this way.

Now it is noteworthy that in the tradition of Christian worship, as this has been "reformed" in those bodies which were affected by the Reformation movement, this worship of God does in fact include the preaching of the gospel. The sacrament of the Lord's Supper is the chief Christian act of worship and it is so regarded, at least in theory, by all Christians. But it is also true that with the ministration of the sacrament must be associated the proclamation of Christ as Lord. It is this proclamation which gives the meaning to the sacrament —here is the story which explains what is happening, here is the Word preached which gives point to the Word enacted. The fact that the pulpit is at one side does not mean that it is unimportant. It is not correct to say that liturgical worship is alien to that kind of Christian worship which finds place, as a central element, for the declaration of the *kerygma*. On the contrary, the two go together. Christ the Word is preached so that he may be received "by faith with thanksgiving." The two go together; and it is a significant element in the new liturgical emphasis found in both "Catholic" and "Evangelical" churches that it is more and more recognized that they go together. We may be on the way to recovering something of the wholeness of Christian worship which has been broken during the past few centuries.

The greatest objective in liturgical worship is the creation of the new man in Christ. This means the creation of the "liturgical man," as some recent Roman and Anglican writers have put it. The man who is shaped and molded by his continuing participation in the round of Christian liturgical worship is the man who comes gradually to be informed by the spirit which animates and governs the liturgy—and that spirit is nothing other than response to the gospel of Christ, made known and communicated through the preaching of the gospel, but not through *verbal* symbols alone; the response becomes effective through the whole action which includes mind and body, will and emotions, in an offering to God in union with his brethren.

The man who is shaped by the liturgy is a man whose life is marked by an awareness of the mystery of existence, grounded in the mystery of God, but who yet has been made partaker of the revelation of the mystery which was made in Christ and which is the hidden heart of the Church's being. He is the man whose inner life is ordered in accordance with the rhythm of the Church's commemoration of Christ. He is the man whose "conversation," whose manner of living, is with Christ, and with God in Christ, and with God in Christ in the fellowship of the Holy Spirit which we call the Holy Church. And this takes place because he is the man who is so informed by the whole ethos of the total liturgical action that he is himself caught up into it and finds it reproduced in himself.

The Holy Communion is the central focus of Christian prayer and worship; it is *the* Liturgy, all other services being ancillary to it. Hence it is appropriate for us here to consider the meaning of this action of Christian worship as the historical tradition of Christianity has understood it, always remembering that our primary concern is to show how this action is related to the kerygmatic proclamation, the preaching of the gospel of God in Jesus Christ for man's wholeness.

In such an analysis it is right to start with the truth that the Eucharist is essentially a divine action into which our human action is caught up. This is why it can be the enacting of the gospel, for the gospel is centered not in what man has done but in what God has done. The human response to Christ in faith comes *after* the proclamation of Christ as embodying the divine self-expressive action which we call incarnation. So in the Eucharist the human actions, which are of course the *obvious* part of the sacrament, are the consequence of, and are themselves enfolded in, the divine action in which God makes available to his people what theologians call "the benefits of Christ."

The Eucharist is first of all something done, rather than something said or something thought about.

Wherefore, O Lord and heavenly Father, according to the institution of thy dearly beloved Son, our Saviour Jesus Christ, we thy humble servants do celebrate and make here before thy divine majesty, with these thy holy gifts which we now offer unto thee, the memorial thy Son hath commanded us to make, having in remembrance his blessed Passion and precious Death, his mighty Resurrection and glorious Ascension, rendering unto thee most hearty thanks for the innumerable benefits procured unto us by the same.

These words, from the Prayer of Consecration in the American Book of Common Prayer, set the right note for our thinking about the eucharistic action. Here, in this celebration, is a memorial which the New Testament tells us that Christ commanded us to make. In our present context, we are not concerned with the details of New Testament study in respect to eucharistic origins; hence it will suffice to say that there can be no question that in some genuine sense the sacrament does have its origin in the actions of our Lord himself and that the primitive Christian community as it met for the "breaking of bread" believed that it was thus established by him for his "continual remembrance."

Thus the Eucharist, as an action, is an action which "remembers." However it may be with us today, it is important that we recognize that for a first-century Jew "memorial" did not mean reverie about past events; it meant the act of vitally recalling into the present that which those events achieved for the Jewish people. So for the early Christians the eucharistic action was not simply a mental recollection of Christ and especially of his sacrificial death; it was God's bringing the life of Christ and his sacrificial death into the present experience of the Christians who celebrated the sacrament. But our use of the words "sacrificial death" brings before us a further aspect of the action. As Luther saw, and as Gustav Aulen has recently argued in a study of the eucharistic doctrine of Luther, the fact that by a memorial action Christ becomes present in the sacramental rite means that his sacrifice itself becomes present also, for we have to do with the "whole Christ" and the "whole Christ" includes all that he experienced in the days of his flesh. There can, of course, be no repetition of Calvary, neither are we to think any new sacrifice of our Lord is being offered by us. The Reformers rightly denied such views. But when we obey his command and bless the bread and wine, our Lord in making himself present to us his people makes present to us also the "one oblation of himself once offered" on Calvary. Here we have a sense in which we can quite properly speak of the Eucharist as a sacrificial action.

Christ becomes *present* in the action. He is present, of course, to our faith, which is "the means whereby we receive the sacrament"; but this does not imply, as some have thought, that his presence is an imagined one or that it is simply a presence in a kind of mental attitude which the breaking of bread and the sharing of the cup awaken in us. It is a true and genuine presence, as Dr. Donald Baillie so well argued in his *Theology of the Sacraments*. The exact mode of it we cannot describe, but the reality of it we know as we "feed on him in our heart, by faith, with thanksgiving." There could be no presence more "real" than a presence to faith. And that reality is indelibly associated with the bread and wine which are used according to Christ's own action at the Last Supper, so that in receiving them we may say, as the Church has always said, that we receive "the spiritual food of the body and blood of Christ," and that we receive this "to our great and endless comfort," or strengthening.

Finally, a true communion is established in the Lord's Supper between Christ and those who are his members, his people, his Christians. They receive his life in the sacrament; and at the same time that this brings them into true communion with him, it always establishes a communion among the members themselves. As Christ's people, his Christians, they are brought into the most intimate relationship possible one with another by reason of their being made fellow-participants in the life of Christ made available for them in the eucharistic meal.

It is in this way that we can see, summing up the last few

paragraphs, that the Lord's Supper, like the proclaiming of the gospel itself, is the declaration of a divine action, although this time the proclamation is not in words but in something done. It is a making present, by the operation of the Holy Spirit, of Christ himself in the fullness of his risen life—a risen life in which (as Wesley's hymn so beautifully puts it) "those dear tokens of his passion, still his dazzling body bears," a victorious life which yet was sacrificed or offered to God to the point of death for the wholeness of men. It is a true presence of the Lord of the gospel, as by faith his people open their hearts to receive him into their lives. It is a communion which unites God and man, and man and man, in the person of Christ whom the gospel declares and the sacrament imparts.

Now nothing that we have said thus far about the meaning of the Eucharist is alien either to the general "Catholic" or to the whole "Reformed" tradition. If once we get behind the prejudices and tastes of this or that group of modern Christians, and try to discover what the great continental reformers like Luther and Calvin—yes, and like Zwingli, too, for he has been much misunderstood and misinterpreted by many of those who have claimed to interpret his teaching —not to mention the English reformers with their rather closer contact with the Catholic tradition, we shall find that with varying emphases and in varying idiom, they were all of them intent on saying something very like the summary outline which I have just given. One of the heartening things about recent theological investigation has been the way in which this essential agreement is more and more being brought to light.

Father George Tyrrell, that tragic figure in the Roman

Catholic Modernist Movement, once wrote that the Christianity of the future would consist in "the Eucharist and charity." It is not quite clear what precisely Tyrrell meant by this moving phrase, for his remark was made only in passing; but we can on our part take the words as suggesting how, in a deep sense, the whole content of our Christian faith, understood as our response to the gospel of Christ, may be summed up. For the Eucharist does gather together the basic themes of the gospel; and "charity" or life-in-love which gives itself generously to others, is the quality which marks Christian life, the hidden and expressed meaning of the life of the man who is "in Christ." *Eucharist* leading to *charity,* and all of this because of the response to and entrance into life lived in and with Chrst: certainly there could hardly be a better definition of Christianity.

Let us now notice that *Eucharist* is Greek for "thanksgiving." May we not say that it is no accident that the name commonly used for the sacrament in most traditional thinking and writing witnesses to the grateful response which men make to that which the gospel proclaims? So we come to consider what it is that *we* do in making that grateful response. What are the *human* actions which are gathered up and enfolded in the divine action which the sacrament essentially is?

First of all, we offer. The Eucharist is a thank-offering. It is a grateful offering of "ourselves, our souls and bodies"; it is an offering of thanksgiving in that it is the "continual remembrance of the sacrifice of the death of Christ"; it is the Church's offering of itself to God in gratitude for Christ's "benefits."

Man has ever sought to find something worthy to offer

to God, something which would express his adoration, his contrition, his love for his Creator and his sovereign Lord. This explains what seem to us the strange and horrible sacrificial rites of primitive peoples; they are seeking to find something that they may present to their god—their *best* gift, even if it meant the offering of the bravest man, or of a treasured possession, or of some animal of flawless quality. We need to have the insight and the imagination to see that behind these barbaric rites there is something that is right: there is this desire planted in man's heart to give to the divine reality, however conceived, that which is worthy of him. Yet we can see also that as men grow in understanding they come slowly to recognize that such offerings are unworthy of God and that the only really satisfactory offering must be the self-giving of man himself, fully surrendered to God. But that which man knows he should do, he also knows he cannot do. And here the action of God in the man Jesus Christ comes into context. For in Christ, one Man did offer himself fully and completely in obedience to the will of God, in a self-surrender which led him to the Cross. The whole of our Lord's life was a giving; and that giving reached its climax on Calvary where it was, so to say, thrown high to God the Father and thrust down deep into the world of men. In the Eucharist Christ's Church "re-calls" that supreme sacrificial action, "remembers" it before the Father, saying in the words of a well-loved hymn:

> Look Father, look on his anointed face,
> And only look on us as found in him.

No Christian thinkers have understood this truth about the Lord's Supper better than John and Charles Wesley, who in their eucharistic hymns, and especially in the hymns of Charles, speak nobly of the way in which we "plead" the sacrifice which was once and for all accomplished on Calvary. Certainly there is danger in our using sacrificial language about Christ's death and about the sacrament in which that death is recalled. But if we never forget that Calvary is the culmination of a whole life of obedience, self-surrender, and self-giving to God, and that the medieval sayings are right which speak of "the whole life of Christ as the mystery of the Cross" and of the sacrifice of Christ as "not the death but the willingness of him who dies," we are delivered from this danger so far as our Lord's death is concerned. Similarly, if we constantly bear in mind that the Eucharist has sacrificial reality only insofar as it makes Jesus, in the fullness of his life, present to his people, while at the same time it calls forth from them the whole-hearted surrender of themselves in Christ and by Christ's grace to the Father, we shall not fall into error in describing the eucharistic action as sacrificial in nature.

The Church offers that which it is, the Body of Christ, that it may more fully and really become what it is, the Body of Christ. So St. Augustine saw; and so many centuries later John Calvin taught in his treatise on the sacrament of the Lord's Supper. That is one side of the Eucharist, then: the offering, the oblation, the pleading, the sacrificial side of it. But there is another side; and that is the second part of the human action in the Eucharist.

There is the receiving. For the Lord's Supper is the way in which, by our Lord's ordinance, we are fed by him, strengthened by him, nourished in him, sent forth in his power to carry him into the world of everyday life and experience. First there is the offering, which the Church can perform only as it is identified in faith and obedience with the Lord who in the deepest understanding of the Eucharist is himself the One who offers; then there is the receiving, as the members of Christ's Body are incorporated anew into their Lord and are fed with "the bread that cometh down from heaven," even with Christ himself. Whatever may be our theory of the mode of that feeding, whatever may be our understanding of the nature of the presence of Christ in the Holy Communion, the *fact* of it remains; and it is so real and so universal an experience of Christians that we need not dwell on it further.

The Lord's Supper is integrally bound up with the proclamation of the gospel, so that either one of them without the other is truncated and partial. It is not that the gospel adds anything to the sacrament, or the sacrament adds anything to the gospel; it is simply that they *belong* together, that together they *make one thing*—and that one thing is the Lord Jesus Christ, in whom God so richly and truly dwelt for the wholeness of men. This is why the normal worship of the Christian should be the combined ministry of Word and sacrament. Sunday by Sunday, as Christ's people come to worship God, they should both hear the Word and receive the sacrament; and by those two, which are really one, be built up in Christ their Lord and their life, by whom, through Word and sacrament, they are nourished and strengthened for Christian witness as "faithful soldiers and servants of Christ, until their life's end."

6.

THE

NEW

SPIRIT

Bishop Lightfoot of Durham, the noted nineteenth-century
New Testament scholar, once remarked that in his judgment
"there is nothing so dangerous as the desire to make everything right and tight." He then went on to say that he had
found that his faith "suffered nothing by leaving a thousand
questions open," so long as he was "convinced on two or
three main lines." It is the "two or three main lines" with
which we have been concerned here; and there is nothing
but danger, I believe, for Christian thought in attempting,
or even in desiring, "to make everything right and tight."
There are areas in which we cannot hope to have all the answers, although at the same time it is incumbent upon us
to apply to our Christian faith such reason as we possess.
F. J. A. Hort, the associate of Lightfoot's in the famous
"Cambridge three," wrote that "there can be no surer sign
of decrepitude and decay in faith than the prevalent nerv-
ousness about naming and commending reason"; and it

is certainly true that whenever men reject the right of reason to look at and study the Christian faith, they are inviting disaster.

The liberalism which is now so much decried had at its very heart such a deep concern for reason applied to faith. Doubtless, in some few of its representatives, it tended towards a minimizing of certain distinctive Christian tenets; doubtless it could lead, and with some few did lead, to what has been described as a "watering-down" of such affirmations as those concerning the sinfulness of man, the deity of Jesus Christ, and the transcendence of God. Yet even among those who manifested such tendencies, there was a concern for maintaining the other side of these affirmations; there was an insistence that man is made in the image of God, that Christ is one with his human brethren, and that God is at work in his world here and now. And these are also important aspects of Christian truth, always in need of emphasis. Above all, the liberal school sought to relate the whole world to God and God to the whole world.

As we take a long historical view, it is obvious that in addition to the influence of many different cultural factors and the pressure of historic events, one reason for the rejection of "liberalism" was that in the dialectic of thought a reaction was due. To the extent that these movements of the late nineteenth and early twentieth centuries went to one extreme, to that extent we might have expected what has indeed happened—the reaction has gone to the other extreme. In one sense, we may say, the reaction has been salutary. And yet it might be argued that in many ways "liberalism" and "modernism" were more on the "side of the angels" than the reaction has been or is. Our reason for this is that it is increasingly our conviction that narrow biblical specialization, introspective theologizing, and self-conscious "religiosity" are really less in line with the high purposes of traditional Christian thinking than was the profound, if sometimes overextended, broadmindedness and generosity of spirit in the preceding period. At any rate, we believe that now is the time for a return to a genuine middle road—which is yet not a "middle road" if by this is meant a compromised and compromising way, but rather a positive recognition of the essential nature of the religio-theological enterprise as a whole.

What we really need is a new spirit. What we need is a deeply religious, theologically oriented, and traditionally grounded understanding of Christianity, which is yet prepared to look critically at the inherited system of Christian thought, ready to subject it to the most careful examination, and above all concerned to restate it in such terms as shall make sense to men and women who are living today. There is no value in fancy adaptations of Christian faith or practice which will seek to cut these down to "what Jones can take"; we cannot be authentically Christian and at the same time bow before every superficial demand of modern men and women. Our present need is a reverent yet radical evaluation of the whole Christian tradition which will be determined, on the one hand, to preserve continuity with our Christian past, but which, on the other hand, will not think that that past in and of itself settles all our problems. It is to a statement of such a position that I invite your attention, in the conviction that a clear statement of the case will be in itself the best apologetic for it.

What are the essential elements in this position? Perhaps

they may be summarized briefly in this way: the maintenance of the great central affirmations of historical Christianity as a faith centering in the person and work of Jesus Christ
as the incarnate, risen, and ever-living Lord; and at the same
time a welcome to new knowledge from whatever source it
may come, with a readiness for continual reinterpretation
of these central affirmations in the light of the new situations
in which the Church finds itself. Thus we have freedom
of enquiry coupled with loyalty to the essence of the tradition; we have openness of mind combined with abiding
faith in the gospel's Lord.

We must all admit that there is an enormous authority behind the central affirmations of Christian faith. They are
grounded in Scripture, they have been tested by the Church's
experience, they are confirmed by reason, and they may be
validated by their results in Christian life. But we ought to
remember that the authority is a genuine *consensus*; it is not
an imposed and coercive *imperium*. And old story about
two Christian theologians illustrates the point: one said that
he believed the faith because the Church taught it; the
other that he believed it because it was true. Yet surely
these two should never be separated, for the Christian
Church is concerned with truth and it worships its Lord as
the Truth; and for this reason whatever is true and whoever is "of the truth" should be able to find in the Church a
cordial and generous welcome. And the Christian gospel,
while in itself given once-for-all—since it centers in the
life of Jesus Christ and in his abiding significance—is
capable of application to all kinds of situations in all kinds of
cultures; it is capable of statement, theologically speaking, in
many different forms and in most diverse idiom, without any

damage to the declaration which it makes. Unless we believe this, surely we have an altogether provincial view of the meaning of the faith which we profess and the Lord in whom we have that faith.

Orthodoxy, both traditional and "neo-," has hold of highly important truths. It sees rightly that where much modern religion has failed is in that it has broken with the continuity of Christian thought and experience. It understands that once this heritage is forgotten or lost, there is little left to religion save emotion, some kind of vague "cosmic consciousness," moral imperatives, and social enthusiasm. Orthodoxy has recognized that any religion which is to be effectual in the lives of men must be grounded in history, conveyed through institutions, and continuous with its past. Furthermore, it has insisted—and rightly—that Christianity is a faith and not a philosophical or ethical system; it is a faith in which affirmations are made about an historical person in whom God is believed to be specially at work; it has insisted that we have to do with a tradition which has been nourished by the lives of holy men and women, by saints and scholars, but which is based upon the gospel, whose grounding is in the scriptural record and witness and which therefore cannot exist without constant reference to that "deposit" of God's self-revelation.

But at the same time there is a danger that orthodoxy, with all these values, will become sterile, purely verbal, unless it is constantly open to investigation, always ready to hear criticism, and unfailingly seeking to bring itself into relationship with the new situations in which men find themselves. This is why there must be freedom for the scholar to enquire into the historical problem of Christian origins, for example; why there must be freedom to think through once again what in the Christian tradition is "central" and what is "peripheral" (to use Professor Burnaby's words which I quoted in an earlier lecture); why there must be freedom to reconceive and restate what is then seen to be of the essence of the faith. Such freedom can be allowed in the Christian Church precisely because any questionings as to the manner in which the divine fire came into the world in Jesus Christ, and any analysis of the essential significance of that coming, cannot deny the fact that the fire did come and that it is burning still.

One reason for a good deal of contemporary, unthinking Christian conservatism is simply fear. And the fear is a faithless fear. We have all heard it said that *if* we give up this or that, *if* we attempt to think through once again this or that article of faith, *if* we have an open mind about this or that supposed historical assertion in the creedal formulae, we inevitably imperil the *whole* Christian position. One can only reply that if the Christian position is based upon what will not bear the most thorough investigation of its detailed particulars, it is not worth maintaining. Surely the gospel, and the faith which the gospel awakens, will not be destroyed by a knowledge, as accurate as we can make it, of how they originated. The interpretation of the significance of Jesus Christ in the light of Christian experience is a given fact, quite as much as is the historicity of the Lord himself. The justification of that interpretation is that it makes sense of the traditions about him, that it is true to the living experience of his presence and power, that it illuminates the whole field of history, and that it throws light on all nature and life. We do not need to fear that it will be overthrown by the honest and reverent effort of biblical critics to determine what actually happened to give rise to it. What is again needed to-day—and remember that I am attempting to describe a position which will regard Christianity as a living, growing tradition, continuous with its past yet open to the present, ready for critical investigation and concerned to restate the faith for those who live in our own day—is precisely this fearless attitude about the faith, this honest effort at enquiry, and this constant willingness to relate the gospel to the changed world of a new age.

This way of looking at Christianity is indeed very different from a good many popular contemporary versions of the faith. Let me give an example. A widely read book by Harry Blamires is entitled *The Faith and Modern Error.* Mr. Blamires has the following words:

The young of today are looking for complete systems. Hence the appeal of Marxism and Jehovah's Witnesses. Hence too, we may admit, the resurgence of Thomism as a living influence upon the young. . . . [He then goes on to speak of the attitude of mind which would] distinguish between credible and incredible doctrines as hopelessly and ludicrously out of date. The young clamour for a system. Picking and choosing . . . means nothing except to those brought up to it. The one thing we can most safely and certainly say of modernism is that it is no longer modern.

Now, the writer of these words appears to be saying that because many today, and especially as he thinks "the young," are looking for "complete systems," the Church is bound to provide one such system; and evidently it is to provide that system without regard to questions of truth, of fact, of credibility to the rational mind. To be concerned for these latter matters is for Mr. Blamires to be "hopelessly out of date." The extraordinary thing is that in Mr. Blamires' attack on "modernism" we have a horrifying example of very *bad* and *wrong* modernism veiling itself as ancient orthodoxy. Here we are urged to make a simple accommodation to the demands of what certainly we may call the *unthinking* members of our generation; we have an eager willingness to accept without question what appears to be their desire for an authoritative totalitarian system which has no respect for truth; we have, in fact, a shocking submission to the worst aspects of the modern mind.

We have seen in an earlier chapter that in our concern for rethinking, reconceiving, restating, we must be aware of and concerned with contemporary ideas; yet we are never to regard the patterns of thought (or what, following Professor Alexander, we styled the "ordinary knowledge" of our time), as if these gave us the last word, the final criterion, the absolute standard. But this is exactly what Mr. Blamires and others who think like him are prepared to do. It is one of the tragedies of the present situation in Christian thought that so many popular apologists take just this position. There can be little question that it is this attitude which prevents the more thoughtful and the more honest men and women of our time from feeling any real respect for Christianity. Perhaps some of those within the Church may delight in such scandalous disregard for the claims of truth; perhaps some who are in retreat from the world may come to embrace a Christianity so presented. But it is shameful that Christian spokesmen should speak like this, in the name of the Lord who, as Tertullian once said, "called himself not tradition but the Truth."

On the contrary, those who hold the view that I am describing, will say that no matter what modification or reinterpretation may be required from time to time, the central assertions of Christianity, its gospel and the faith which the gospel awakens, stand firm. We are not obliged to retreat into the kind of obscurantism which Mr. Blamires and his friends commend. For in holding fast to the revelation of God in Christ, brought to us through the Church, as supreme, adequate, definitive, we are led to see that there can be continuing expansion, development, restatement, reconception, without peril of any essential loss. The gospel may be exposed to all the winds of God, for it is limitless in its range, sure of its ground, and able to assimilate and use everything that is good and true and lovely. The gospel is the truth which makes men *free*.

In a recent careful review of several studies lately published about Charles Darwin and his influence, Professor Gillispie, of Princeton University, noted that with most of the Victorian "rationalists" and "agnostics," the "decisive factor" in their turning from the Christian faith was "in no case the findings of science." Rather, he said, "in every case it was an ethical revulsion from doctrines of the atonement, everlasting damnation, original sin, and an omnipotent God who permits evil." And he went on to observe that "a theology which had drowned in rivers of vulgar evangelical piety, or which had blown away on the high ecclesiastical winds of Tractarian romance" was likely to be of little help to such men. Mr. Gillispie's last words are somewhat unguarded and they probably require considerable qualification; nonetheless, it is not without significance that an expert in the field believes that what was lacking for most of the Victorian worthies about whom he is writing was a presentation of Christian faith which would not be intellectually absurd or morally offensive. Unhappily, the few Christian thinkers of the time who were attempting such a presentation of Christianity were either rejected or neglected by the great mass of churchmen.

In our own day, the situation is of course very different. But yet it is still sadly true that large numbers of our more thoughtful contemporaries are repelled from the Church because they find in it what looks to them like sheer unthinking obscurantism, a shockingly immoral attitude towards truth (of which Mr. Blamires' book is an example), and a cavalier disregard of patent fact about the world in which we live. There can be little doubt that one reason for Christian failure here has been the narrowing of the significance of the gospel's proclamation of God in Christ with its theological corollary in the dogma of the Incarnation. This point must be developed.

The Incarnation of God in Christ is not only the supreme means by which God unites himself with men and thereby makes them "sharers in the divine nature," as II Peter puts it; it is also the signal clue for our understanding of the whole of creation and the whole of human experience. Cardinal Bérulle once said that the Incarnation "is the condition, the work, and the mystery wherein God reigns, and whereby he reigns, in his creatures." So it is that the Christian faith in Jesus Christ as God's revelation of himself is in the closest relation with the whole process in which he appears. We must be willing to recognize that the world in which we live is an order which everywhere expresses, although in varied mode and degree, the one eternal Reality who is present and active throughout, but in no sense identical with, the creation; and, in consequence, that in Christ there has appeared the focus of this process and the crowning manifestation of God as self-expressive in it. There is no absolute break between the wider self-expression of God which classical theology regarded as the operation of the Eternal Word or God Self-Expressive, and Jesus Christ and the community of which, as the late Professor C. C. J. Webb once put it, he is "the founder and guide"; that community which, as Professor Webb went on to say, is "the organ and vehicle of his risen life." In theological language, the Eternal Word, the *Logos,* "by whom all things were made" and who is "the light lightening every man," has in Christ achieved actualization in genuinely human terms.

Now what has all this to do with preaching the gospel? Very much, I think. For if in all the good realities of the world of nature, of history, and of human experience, the divine Word expresses himself, the whole of it may be regarded as preparation for Christ: it is a *praeparatio evangelica.* In him the Word, ever "coming" to men, ever "given" to them and "indwelling" them, however partially and inadequately that may be, "comes" so richly to men in a Man that he overflows this instance of humanity and lifts the whole human race to a new level of existence. We might call that new level God-in-manhood; or better and more scripturally, we should speak of it as life-in-Christ. Into that new life men are taken as they respond in faith to the proclamation of the gospel and are incorporated into the

Christian fellowship. D. M. Edwards, a now almost forgotten Welsh theologian of the earlier years of this century, put the point in striking words:

Jesus Christ is the living meeting-point of heaven and earth, of God and man, the keystone of the cosmic arch, the culmination at once of emergent evolution working 'upwards' and of the divine self-impartation working 'downwards,' at once the summit of human achievement and the supreme gift of love whereby God gives 'his very self and essence all divine.'

The gospel of Christ which we preach is the proclamation of something that is "ever old, ever new." It is old, in that it is the same Word who from the beginning has sustained the creation and unceasingly has disclosed himself in it "in divers manners," who in "these last days" has focally expressed himself in the manhood of Jesus Christ. It is new, in that this focal expression of God in Christ is the opening of a hitherto unknown possibility of life for men; as St. John Damascene said long ago, this is "a new thing, the newest of all new things, the only really new thing under the sun." So our Lord is a genuine emergent and not a mere resultant; in him we find God's life lived in a true human life, to the end that we men may be participant in the divine life expressed in him.

In consequence of this claim, our preaching of the gospel has a cosmic sweep. We must acknowledge the real measure of divine revelation and grace which is to be found in the non-Christian religions and in any other place where men meet that which commands their fullest and purest allegiance. No man has insisted on this more vigorously than Baron von Hügel, who with all his deep faith in the fullness of our Lord's embodiment of God, was yet ever ready to maintain that in other religious traditions, and likewise in science, art, philosophy, ethics, as well as in the simple hum-drum experiences of daily life, God in some way and to some degree has been found and known. The Christian assertion is not that Christ *destroys* these other manifestations; it is that he *fulfills, corrects, explains* them for what they are. The history of religion is what Professor Webb, whom we have already quoted, once called "the story of a single Incarnation of God in humanity, culminating in the life and death of Jesus Christ, and in his risen life," with "the capacity eventually to assimilate and incorporate the whole religious experience of mankind."

This perspective redeems the gospel we are commissioned to preach from triviality and from parochialism, even while it still gives that gospel "a local habitation and a name." The late Canon Quick spoke of this in moving words:

The Christian . . . who finds, even in a primitive or possibly corrupt religion, points of contact with his own faith, is not a relativist or a syncretist, tacking together a muddled theology or patchwork; rather he is a disciple who knows so clearly him whom he has believed, that he can recognize the tokens of his presence in any Nazareth which so-called orthodoxy has despised. The Buddhist's sympathy with the pain of the world, the Hindu's sense of the unchanging stability of the Eternal, the Moslem's realization of international comradeship, the Confucian's appreciation of social morality, and . . . the sacrifices of scientific workers in the quest of truth and human welfare [and today, may we not add the Communist's concern for social justice, the humanist's insistence on the value of right self-realization of man's capacities, and the secularist's recognition of the non-religious goods in human experience?] give to the Christian a fresh revelation of the Light that lighteth every man, and of the Word made flesh. . . . The Christ is the human Saviour whom men have sought and partially found in the persons of Sakyamuni, Mohammed, Confucius, and many another sage and saint, prophet and reformer, who has followed and pointed the way towards the one true God. But the Christ is found fully only in One who is even more than the Christ, because his Cross is proved to be the very wisdom and power of God himself.

It is against this background, with this understanding of Christianity, this apprehension of the truth in the "orthodox" position, and yet this belief in the necessity for the "modernist" attitude, that the preaching of the gospel can make sense today. The gospel is the proclamation that God is active in the Man Jesus, is self-expressed there, for the wholeness of men. It is this which we are to preach. But we preach it with corollaries that are intimately and immediately its own. Let us set down these corollaries:

That God is our Father, the creator and sovereign ruler of all things visible and invisible, material and spiritual;

That Jesus Christ is his Son and our Lord; that as incarnate Word of God he is that One in whom true God dwells truly in true Man; that for us men and for our wholeness he lived a genuine human life, was crucified for us, and is now alive for evermore;

That in the Spirit known through him we respond to the Father through the Son; and that we worship the three in the unity of the one Godhead;

That we are baptized unto forgiveness of our sins and thereby made members of the one holy catholic and apostolic Church, to be nourished in the life of Christ given in

Holy Communion and to share in the fellowship of the faithful in heaven and in earth;

That we look for the life of the world to come, confidently trusting in God's victory over sin, evil, and death, and our entrance into his never-ending Kingdom.

All this is in fact but one thing; it is the setting for, the meaning of, and the consequences which follow upon, the gospel which we proclaim. Anything beyond this is in the nature of optional, peripheral, "indifferent" belief; and it is wrong (or at least so I think) for us to insist upon such beliefs as a condition for entrance into the Christian community of response in faith. Furthermore, those who now belong with us in acceptance of this gospel and these corollaries, ought to have reasonable freedom to interpret the *how* of the historical *credenda* in a fashion meaningful to them, provided always that their interpretation does not negate the faith by which the Christian fellowship lives. Peter Meiderlin, in words that are usually attributed to Melancthon, gave us the well-known maxim which applies here: "unity in things essential, liberty in things unessential, charity in all things both essential and unessential."

We often unduly complicate the whole business of preaching Christ, and the whole matter of Christian discipleship too, by a kind of theological intransigeance. As a theologian I cannot think that theology is unimportant; I believe that thinking about the gospel and the faith, and the best possible thinking, is utterly necessary. And yet should we not all agree that the big things of the gospel and the big things of the faith are really relatively simple and plain? We shall always need theology, and it must be the best theology we can produce; but, on the other hand, there is a sense in which we should ever sit loose to theology, remembering that the "one thing needful" is the gospel itself and the faith which it awakens in the sons of men, remembering too that the articles of belief should be, in the words of Erasmus which I previously quoted, as few as are necessary.

In the long run, our *credo* is our *amo*; what we really *believe* is what we really *love*. What we call *the* faith is but an articulation of the act of faith, and that means our love, what we desire and yearn for with all our heart and soul and mind and strength, what we give ourselves to, in utter self-donation and self-commitment, what we are prepared to die for and what even now in this present time we are prepared to live by. We need in our preaching both simplicity and depth: simplicity of statement and simplicity of speech, depth of dedication and depth of awareness; above all we need sensitivity and devotion.

APPENDIX A:
TEACHING
CHRISTIAN FAITH
AND ETHICS

Today it is very important, all would agree, that members of the Church should be taught the Christian faith and instructed in Christian ethics. For it is necessary that the faith of the Church, as this has been articulated during the two thousand years of Christian history in the form of theological statements, should be made known to the people; it is equally necessary that the developed principles of Christian life, in respect to devotional practice and in terms of daily conduct, should be taught. In other words, it is necessary that every effort should be made to create an instructed church-membership and to develop an intelligent interest in the discussion of religious questions. Indeed, it may be well to reiterate that the whole enterprise of Christian education is of quite special importance today if we wish to have an informed laity and if we wish to secure for the preaching office of the ministry that particular place which belongs to it and it alone.

My belief, for what it is worth, is that this teaching and instructing can be done much more effectively in the parish house, in the church hall and the like, at sessions specifically arranged for the purpose, rather than in the course of divine worship. One of my former colleagues has coined the phrase: "every parish a school of theology." This is a sound position, although I should wish to have it read "every parish a school of Christian faith, devotion, and life." What this ought to mean for the working parson is that in the planning of his program for the congregation, some genuine opportunity will be provided for such instruction and that this will be regarded as a normal part of parish procedure. Unless there is both a place and a planned scheme for instruction of this sort in the parish program a real opportunity will be missed to strengthen the members of our congregation. What is even worse, the people committed to our care will be deprived of one of their rights, which is that they be thus informed and edified in the things of Christ.

This is being realized increasingly today. It is one of the remarkable developments of recent years in American Christianity that more and more parishes, of all denominations, are establishing schools of religion, "parish institutes," or special series "of classes," which meet regularly for several weeks or even several months; and these are marked by thoughtful planning and high seriousness on the part of the clergy and on the part of the congregation.

To take a single example, last year I had the privilege of participating in one of these schools in a small university town, where in a parish of about one thousand members over

two hundred persons (including a goodly number of interested "enquirers" who had heard of the program through
a carefully planned advertising campaign) attended eight
night sessions, held from eight until ten o'clock, with a choice
among eight different courses, dealing with theological, ethical, historical, devotional, and scriptural subjects. It is of
course true that this particular parish had unique opportunities for drawing on experts in the field who are experienced
teachers. But however it is to be done, there is something
here that greatly needs to be done. The people hunger for
such instruction, although often they cannot articulate this
need.

Such a parish school can concentrate on one subject for
the entire period of operation, with a single session which is
attended by all who are interested. Or the school can be
divided into smaller groups each with its individual leader,
if such leadership is available. Or it can combine the two
methods by having first a general session for one hour and
after that a number of smaller groups for a second hour.
Each of these schemes has its advantages; on the whole the
last is probably best, since it provides for a certain variety
in the over-all program and makes it possible for those who
attend not only to take part in one large meeting where the
whole group is stimulated by consideration of a single topic
over a considerable period of time, but also to share in
special "interest groups" which will give them the opportunity to follow up lines of thought that particularly interest
them or to explore problems that are peculiarly relevant to
their own needs and concerns.

As the result of a fairly large experience in such work I
have come to believe that there are two absolute necessities

in arranging a parish school of this kind. The first is that a nominal fee be charged for attendance, although arrangements may, of course, be made for those who cannot afford even a very small payment. The reason for this charging of a fee is quite simple: people tend to value, to take seriously, and to be ready to work at, something for which they must make some payment, however small it is. They tend to regard lightly and to dismiss as of little importance something which costs them nothing. It should be made clear that the money received from such fees will be used for providing refreshments at the close of the sessions or for meeting whatever expenses the school involves—as, for example, the honorarium paid to a visiting lecturer, if there is one, or the cost of lighting the building and providing extra janitorial service. The other necessity is that those who attend shall be expected to do some real preparation for the sessions, usually in the form of a certain amount of reading in a prescribed book or books. It is perfectly possible to find a book which laypeople can understand, and it is equally possible to limit the expected reading to a few chapters from week to week so that those who attend can get their preparation done before the several sessions. Quite apart from the value that such reading has in itself and in securing intelligent participation in the session—and this may be considerable if the selection of books and chapters is carefully made—the fact that such preparation is expected, once again emphasizes both the seriousness of the work of the school and the importance which is being attached by all participants to what it is planned to do.

There is one other point of a practical nature. This is that the pastor who inaugurates such a parish program must not expect that he will have an immediate success, with large and enthusiastic numbers of attendants at the sessions. It is much better, in fact, if he begins in a small way, with a group which is really interested—and there can be no doubt that such persons can be found in any parish. A small group will itself engender further interest, and perhaps even enthusiasm, if there has been careful planning and a persistent concern for what is important and helpful to its members. The school must not be undertaken, that is, as a brief experiment only; it must be a genuine part of a long-range parish program over several years, with the definite intention of continuing the school so that it will be accepted in time as a normal and expected part of the total life of the congregation. In this way, those who at first failed to show any interest may sooner or later come round to showing it; members of the congregation may begin to develop a habit of attendance; and thus a real start will be made in that highly important and yet very difficult enterprise: adult Christian education. It is inconceivable that any parish should neglect this opportunity; each parish, through its responsible agents, should carefully study its own situation and determine how best it can do the job in this respect.

Now to consider some points which seem to me of quite outstanding importance in the conduct of such a school. First, the method of instruction should be direct but informal. It should not consist in what we might call simply "laying down the law." It should be intended to awaken interest, to stimulate questions, to develop insight and understanding. We all know that sheer didacticism is nowadays regarded with suspicion in secular educational circles; and there is no need to introduce it into our schools of religion. Christianity presupposes, and asks, the free and willing response of those who are taught. It is not authoritarian if this means sheer dictation. Indeed, it is worth noting that "authority" means, as the Latin original implies, moral trustworthiness engendered through deep respect for those who are in a position to know. This suggests to us that in teaching our people about the faith, about theology, about Christian devotion, and about Christian duty, our effort should be not to coerce but to lead. The corollary of this over-all approach is freedom for questions, for discussion, and for the exploration by both leader and hearers of the particular matters that are under discussion. Anyone who has been engaged in teaching is well aware of the fact that there is no surer way to kill interest, and we may add no more certain way to destroy the sense of Christian freedom, than by dogmatic teaching in the *worse* sense of the term. Furthermore, if by way of preparation for the meeting, some preliminary reading has been done by the participants, if the leader lets them feel that they are not just "lecture-fodder" but part of the whole enterprise, and if there is insistence on something more than being at the "receiving-end," the discussion and the questions and the desire for further exploration will almost inevitably follow.

In the second place, it should be understood by everyone concerned that schools of religion are not like other schools in at least one respect. They are not being conducted with a graduate diploma in view. Hence there is no absolute necessity for completing fully a prescribed topic; there is no need to "cram" the attendants as if they were preparing for an examination paper. There should be willingness on the part of the leader to follow, so far as may be, the direction of interest of those who are present. Very often the leader may find that some point which he has made in his preliminary presentation will lead eventually into what may appear to be a by-path. But if he is imaginative and ingenious, and especially if he has had a little experience in techniques of teaching, he will be able to handle the new topic and yet at the same time keep the meeting going along the general line which has been laid down or prepared. If the leader is not a good teacher, then he had better learn how to be one.

Again, the leader must not let himself be put in the position, and above all he must not himself seek to get into the position, of being simply a giver of "the answers." Often enough he will know that as a matter of fact he *cannot* give them. He ought to be honest with himself and not easily victimized by that adulation to which some leaders, and particularly some parsons, so readily succumb. Or he may recognize that to some questions there are various possible answers, one of which may especially appeal to a particular person but none of which is final, absolute, and unquestionable. It is far better to admit ignorance, to show openness of mind, than to claim, or seem to claim, omniscience. Above all a leader should beware lest he give the impression that the Church or even God has spoken with infallible authority through his small mind and poor mouth. Such a procedure of leaving questions open is psychologically much more effective than the pretense to omniscience; it also happens to be more honest. Above all, it is in accord with the mind of Christ.

There is a third point to which attention should be given. Of course, we all have our official or quasi-official "authorities": the Bible, the Book of Common Prayer, confessions of faith, the creeds, and so forth. We may and we ought to use them to help our people to understand the things they should know and believe, live and practice, "to their souls' health." But there is more to it than that. What a pastor must desire above all else is that his people may be led to continue their Christian thinking, their Christian praying, their Christian living. The school of religion is not the end, it is only the beginning. If, for example, we have been dealing with some theological topic, in the attempt to present to our people a consequence of the gospel and its meaning such as they are able and ready to understand and accept, we do not want them to stop with our presentation but to go on asking questions and making further explorations for themselves. If we have been discussing with them the principles of Christian morality, we want them to think again and again of the application of those principles to any and every circumstance of their daily lives. If we have been teaching them about the spiritual life, we want them to put into practice the techniques of Christian prayer and to continue in those techniques, growing in grace and in the knowledge and love of God as they constantly seek him in their regular daily devotions.

In other words, we do not want our people to assume that once they have attended the parish adult school they are then in the position of having learned all there is to learn. Surely we can never think of Christian teaching about faith and morals, or about anything else, as a kind of closed enterprise, at the end of which the job is done and we have finally got our people "fixed" where we should like them to be. Rather, a school such as I am describing, and, for that matter, all other Christian teaching, is the opening of doors to new depths and heights of Christian discipleship. It is not the sheer indoctrination of Christian laymen in what is sometimes called "definite Church teaching." We should avoid like the plague any suggestion that the Christian tradition has come to a stop, above all that it has come to a stop with our particular version of it or presentation of it. "God hath yet more light and truth to break forth from his most holy Word."

In my own experience in such parish schools, made possible for me through the kindness of clergy who have invited me to give them some little assistance in planning or conducting instructional sessions, I have made a further discovery. Often persons who are not Christians, or who are Christians in only a nominal sense, will be happy to avail themselves of the opportunity to learn something about Christianity through attendance at such schools. They may not yet be at the stage when they are willing to commit themselves far enough to become members of an "enquirer's class"—valuable and important as these smaller groups are in any congregation. But they do not feel so much "committed" when they are simply attending a series of sessions which have larger attendance and a more general line of approach than the "enquirer's class." I have known laymen to invite a friend who is or who may be interested; I have known other persons who just "turn up" because somehow an announcement has reached them or they have read about the school in the public press. If the sessions are conducted according to good teaching techniques, if there is a free and open spirit on the part of the leader, if there is a readiness to work together and think together about important things, and above all if there is a friendly atmosphere, such persons are quite likely to be sufficiently attracted to return again and again. In the end they may very well be brought to the point where they are ready to affiliate themselves, perhaps partially or perhaps completely, with the Christian Church. In this sense, we can regard these occasions of instruction as being in their own way an evangelistic opportunity in the parish.

Finally, the most important single aspect of teaching or instruction today is the meaning and practice of Christian prayer. Of course, we need more and better teaching about the systematic ordering of the gospel and its corollaries—that is, teaching about the faith as a whole. Of course, the parson has a responsibility to help any who will listen to think their way into the grand theological assertions of the Christian tradition, even while he should also help them to discriminate between primary and secondary elements, between central and peripheral aspects, and to learn how to use the Scriptures according to the best insight of modern biblical scholarship. An understanding of the principles of Christian behavior, which are the inevitable consequences of the life in grace as men respond to the gospel of Christ, is also of supreme importance for men and women who must necessarily live in what it is popular to describe as the subchristian or unchristian world of our own day. Nonetheless, the greatest need today is instruction in the distinctive meaning of *Christian* prayer, and hence in the techniques by which Christians can pray both with the Spirit and with the understanding.

By and large, most earnest Christian people—and we must here include the clergy as well as the laity—are not very well equipped in this respect. Altogether too often prayer is regarded as a kind of gadget by which we can secure what we wish from God; it is, alas, a matter of "pestering the Deity with our petitions," to use a biting phrase of Dean Inge's. One does not deny for one moment either the place or the need for petitionary prayer, when one seriously maintains that this is a very small aspect of the total action of Christian prayer and that it should be *kept* a very small aspect. How many of our people, indeed how many of us in the ordained ministry, really understand that prayer is essentially what St. Thomas Aquinas, following St. John Damascene, said it is: "the elevation of the mind to God"? How many of us know and practice prayer in the order: adoration, thanksgiving, confession, intercession, and petition? How many of us are informed about the practice of meditation and the possibility of mental prayer? How many of us have even thought that we may be called to contemplative or even mystical prayer? Too many have accepted the popular "neo-orthodox" idea that contemplation and mysticism have no place in the Christian life; on the contrary, they have a real place and an important one; and for those who may be called by God to this particular mode of communion with him, there is a great blessing and a wonderful gift. But quite apart from such matters, is it not true that the vast majority of Christian people today simply do not know that prayer is the very air a Christian must breathe, and that a Christian life without some ordered pattern of prayer is not really a Christian life at all?

Surely one of the things that can best be done in schools such as I have described is the teaching of Christian prayer. It is not without significance that hundreds, thousands, even millions of men and women are turning to the cults, to Vedanta, to Zen Buddhism, to "Unity" and "New Thought," to such inane varieties of religion as Christian Science. This is happening precisely because they do not find in the Christian Church, and from the ministers who represent the Church, sincere, intensive, and intelligible instruction in the ways in which men and women may find the true "peace of God" which will enable them to meet the exigencies and vicissitudes of life with high courage, firm faith, and assured trust. We dare not be derelict in our duty at this point, for if we have failed here we have failed almost everywhere.

APPENDIX B:
THE SCOPE
OF PREACHING
AND EVANGELISM

Most of us agree that the preaching of the gospel of Christ is to be distinguished from the teaching of the Christian faith, in the sense of a structure of belief, instruction in theology, and the presentation of the principles of Christian ethics and the technique of the life of devotion. This does not mean, however, that preaching the gospel, proclamation of the Word of God, must necessarily follow one single narrow line—namely, the simple assertion from the pulpit, made over and over again, that Christ is Lord and that he is that One in whom true God acts supremely and decisively for the wholeness of men. Indeed, in the foregoing chapters, especially where we discussed the relationship of preaching to the "given" world in which men live, and some of the problems which we face today in the business of preaching, the effective proclamation of the Word of God was presented as one relating that which God does in Christ to the whole range of human life and experience, to real men in their actual need, to the concrete situations in which our contemporaries find themselves, and to the particular problems which they face today.

Thus we may say that a proper sermon can begin almost anywhere, and may be developed along almost any lines, provided that its *ultimate* starting point is Holy Scripture, in which the record and witness to the gospel are found, and that its final point of reference is always the Lord Jesus Christ, declared to be the Son of God with power. Some sermons may be expository in nature; they may take some passage or passages of Scripture and show how in them the Lord is declared. Other sermons may be drawn from what used to be called, in homiletics classes of thirty years ago, "the life situations" in which men find themselves, where the analysis of this or that problem which our fellow-men must face will lead directly to the gospel as having its startling relevance to the situation. Still again, a sermon may be related to the liturgical action in which it is set; for example, a sermon preached in the course of the celebration of the Holy Communion may take its rise from the Christian action of worship and go on to show who it is that is being worshiped, why he is being worshiped, and the consequences in human life that flow from such worship. There is, then, a great variety of patterns. What binds them together as proclamation of the Church's gospel about Jesus Christ is that in their deepest intention they bring about a meeting of Christ and his people, and that they expect a response in decision, in action, in faith, in obedience, in adoration, in love. And of course, they may have different *secondary* intentions. To give one example, we may on occasion proclaim the Word of God with the specific purpose of securing that Christ's people shall be more faithful, penitent, and regular in their use of the sacramental opportunities which Christ provides in his Church for their growth in grace. But whatever may be this secondary intention, the sermon must have as its primary aim the setting-forth of Christ, the reality of his grace, and the need for a full personal response to him in one fashion or another.

We hear much today about evangelistic preaching. Either inside the church building or outside it, the Word of God must be proclaimed now and again with the *specific* purpose of winning to Christ those who are not yet in any real sense disciples. But this kind of preaching is not the same thing as the Sunday-by-Sunday declaration of the Lord by response to whom the Church lives. It must have a different orientation from the Sunday preaching in the pulpit, given in connection with the action of Christian worship. It is preaching in a very special way and with a very special intention, for it is concerned to win converts to the Lord Jesus Christ, to awaken faith in those who do not have it or to quicken it when it is dead or dying, to refresh those who have become weak in their response to the gospel and have dropped out of the Church or are at best nominal members. Its purpose is to gather in the lost, to convince the doubtful, to increase by our feeble efforts the number of those who, we hope and pray, will become loyal and active participants in the regular life and worship of the Church of Christ.

Evangelistic preaching, then, to be genuinely effective, must center in one or other aspect of the total Christian proclamation, with the use of every honorable device and every respectable technique to drive that aspect home to the hearers. Such preaching is likely to be somewhat selective, in that the evangelist is hardly able to cover the entire range of the gospel's message and corollaries. He must concentrate on the aspect of the gospel which may meet the needs and illuminate the situation of his hearers, showing, from this initial point of contact, how the Lord whom we preach brings help to those who know themselves to be in need of God's grace and how it may bring them into that wholeness of life which it is Christ's will and the Church's responsibility to make available for all the sons of men.

Evangelistic preaching is *always* predicated on the conviction that men and women are in fact in need of God's grace—which is only another way of saying that they are sinners. But this does not mean that such preaching must dwell overmuch on the evil in men; rather, as it seems to me, the preaching is to be focussed primarily on God and his salvation which is the divine answer to the evil in men. To preach the gospel in a truly evangelistic fashion means to try to win men for Christ, not simply to convince men that they are sinful, poor, lonely, and needy. We may start from this latter fact, true as it is; but we must not *concentrate* on it. We are to put the emphasis on the truth that in Christ there is "plenteous grace." The acceptance of the fact that apart from him and from the grace of God in him, men do not have, and cannot have, that fullness of life which it is God's intention that they should have, will then be the starting point for their coming to want the forgiveness, the gracious help, and the new life in Christ which the gospel offers. This means that the *center* of the proclamation remains, what it must always be, Christ our Lord as that One in whom true

God acted for man's wholeness; the center of our preaching cannot be an unhealthy and morbid concentration of all our attention on the sin and weakness of men. Once again, we need above all to emphasize the *positive,* convinced that its attractiveness will bring men to Christ.

AUTHOR'S NOTE

Books and articles cited in the text:

Donald Baillie. *Theology of the Sacraments.* New York: Scribner, 1957.

F. R. Barry. *The Relevance of Christianity.* New York: Scribner, 1931.

F. W. Beare. *The First Epistle of St. Peter.* Oxford: Blackwell, 1947. See p. 106.

Harry Blamires. *The Faith and Modern Error.* London: SPCK, 1956.

John Burnaby. "Bible and Dogma" in *Church Quarterly Review,* April 1958, p. 188.

C. A. Coulson in *An Approach to Christian Education.* London: Epworth Press, 1956. See pp. 41-43.

C. Harold Dodd. *Apostolic Preaching.* New York: Harper's, 1936.

William Porcher DuBose. *Turning Points of My Life.* New York: Longmans Green, 1911.

John Knox. *The Early Church and the Coming Great Church.* Nashville: Abingdon, 1955.

C. S. Lewis, *Miracles.* New York: Macmillan, 1958.

R. C. Moberly. *Ministerial Priesthood.* London: John Murray, 1910.

Derwyn Owen. *Scientism, Man, and Religion.* Philadelphia: Westminster, 1952.

R. Douglas Richardson. *The Gospel of Modernism.* London: Skeffington, 1935. See p. 178.

James Matthew Thompson. *Through Fact to Faith.* London: Edward Arnold, 1912.

Alfred North Whitehead. *Religion in the Making.* New York: Macmillan, 1926.